WITHDRAWN

D1263478

Carleton College Library

Folger Documents of Tudor and Stuart Civilization

WILLIAM LAMBARDE AND
LOCAL GOVERNMENT

FOLGER DOCUMENTS

OF TUDOR AND STUART CIVILIZATION

THIS volume is one of a series of publications of Tudor and Stuart documents that the Folger Library proposes to bring out. These documents will consist of hitherto unprinted manuscripts as well as reprints of rare books in the Folger Library. An effort will be made to choose significant items that will throw light on the social and intellectual background of the period from 1485 to 1715. In response to almost unanimous requests of interested historians, the spelling, punctuation, and capitalization will be modernized in printed texts. In some cases, where the original printing is clear and easily read, texts may be photographically reproduced. The Folger Library is prepared to supply microfilm of original texts to scholars who require a facsimile.

(THE FOLGER SHAKESPEARE LIBRARY IS ADMINISTERED
BY THE TRUSTEES OF AMHERST COLLEGE.)

William Lambarde

AND

Local Government

His "Ephemeris" and Twenty-nine

Charges to Juries and Commissions

EDITED BY

Conyers Read

PUBLISHED FOR

The Folger Shakespeare Library

BY

CORNELL UNIVERSITY PRESS

Ithaca, New York

KD
7550
.L35

Copyright © 1962 by the Folger Shakespeare Library

CORNELL UNIVERSITY PRESS

First published 1962

Library of Congress Catalog Card Number: 62-9961

PRINTED IN THE UNITED STATES OF AMERICA
BY VAIL-BALLOU PRESS, INC.

942.05
L3tw

Preface

OF the two pieces here presented, the late Conyers Read printed the "Ephemeris," with an introduction and notes, in the *Huntington Library Quarterly* in 1952 (XV, 123–158). Later, when the Folger series of historical and literary documents was planned, he proposed that the "Ephemeris," together with the charges to juries, form a volume in it, and at the time of his death in 1959 he had virtually finished his work on the text, notes, and introduction of the charges.

The importance of these manuscripts lies in the nature of William Lambarde's activities and abilities. He was one of the foremost expositors of the Elizabethan judicial system, and for this task he was admirably fitted by training, by the scholarly bent of his mind, perhaps also by his social status among the new gentry sprung from London trade. Even as a young man he must have acquired something of the passionate devotion to good order and of the belief in the dependence of good order upon sound judicial proceedings that is so conspicuous in his later utterances.

It may well have been this devotion that drove him to abandon antiquarian pursuits in favor of a close study of the judicial and law-enforcement systems. His *Duties of Constables*, his *Eirenarcha*, and his *Archion* cover the whole range from

v

petty constable to Star Chamber, the first two being manuals for the guidance of men with small legal learning. Twelve editions of the *Duties* and seventeen of *Eirenarcha,* spread over a forty-year period, demonstrate both the need for such books and the warm acceptance that these met with.

They are practical books, but with Lambarde practice is grounded in theory and theory in history. In the manuscripts here printed one can see how the historian and the theorist applied his knowledge to the day-by-day work of a justice. In the "Ephemeris" we travel the Western Division of Kent with him as he determines cases of bastardy or assault or theft and takes sureties for the keeping of the peace. In the charges, chiefly delivered at Maidstone, he lectures the grand juries on the law's excellence and the happiness of subjects under a rule of law presided over by so enlightened a prince and so loving a mother as Elizabeth. His basic themes recur again and again, presented with a lively versatility of illustration and with fervor, also with patience and tenderness. But he who spares the rod hates the child, and Lambarde lays about him with a will to correct the self-interest, the timidity, the thoughtlessness that hamper the execution of justice and bring on a train of greater ills. He calls the jurors to a realization of their duty to God, their duty to the Queen, their duty to the commonwealth— which are in fact one duty, not three. He enlarges on the growing evils and corruption of the age and exhorts the jurors to save their ancient liberties and the state itself by wielding the sword of justice which they hold in their own hands. Coming to particulars, he enumerates again and again the duties of jurymen and the prevalent faults that threaten the dissolution of society.

The faults that Lambarde condemns in his juries were not new in Elizabeth's reign, though it did not suit his purpose to point this out to his hearers. The faults were known to Bracton in the thirteenth century and are, indeed, inherent in the system of trial by jury. But the insight that Lambarde offers us into the particular difficulties obstructing law enforcement and the judicial process in the quarter sessions of a Kentish town about 1600 is by no means without interest for the historian. Lambarde's very repetitions (understandable enough in a series of addresses to a changing body of hearers) are instructive, for they show what difficulties most disturbed him and what arguments he regarded as most likely to succeed.

How much effect the arguments had we can only guess. It is clear that he attached much importance to them and employed all his art to move his hearers. The rhetoricians enjoined care first for the large structure and then for word and phrase, and Lambarde neglected neither. In the margins of what may have been his first charge to a jury, March 22, 1581/82 (p. 153), he marks the divisions of his matter in formal rhetorical terms, and though this is our only sight of the bones of the structure, the careful planning is everywhere observable. His attention to the smaller elements is evident in the score or two of deletions and interlinings that crowd almost every manuscript page and make a few all but indecipherable. Some changes are stylistic only, appealing to the ear or improving coherence. In a far greater number his objective is more precise expression and more striking emphasis, as a sentence in No. 10 of the quarter sessions charges shows (italics in this transcript represent Lambarde's additions; square brackets, his deletions):

And therefore, omitting to *re*commend the religion and justice of our laws, *two things* which by the only *mention and* naming of them do sufficiently commend themselves, and letting pass all rehearsal of the benefits that do ensue by the diligent observation of the same (the which if any man seeth not he is too too blind: and if he acknowledge not he is utterly froward and willful), I will only propound unto you that *great* fear, *peril*, and danger wherein we stand to have [both the one and the other *of these*] *the benefit of the free* *and familiar use of our country laws* (through our unreverent and careless handling of them) to be *quite and clean removed and* taken from us, *than the which I know no loss (that of the religion of God only excepted) that may fall more heavy or hurtful unto us.*

One can but wonder if Lambarde's careful polishing was of much service to the success of his message when he indulged his taste for long periodic sentences overloaded with parentheses, such as the one just quoted—or the opening of No. 19 (p. 145). Sentences like that are not easily grasped when read. In oral delivery it is hard to believe that they would be persuasive with the Kentish villagers, even though we assume on their part a most respectful attention to the distinguished justice's exhortations. Occasionally Lambarde reaches high eloquence in the best Elizabethan style, as in the opening of the second paragraph of No. 14 (p. 123). But even here the learned lawyer seems to be addressing the wrong audience, and it is not surprising that he effected no notable reform in the attitudes of jurors.

The text here printed is, so far as possible and except for spelling, punctuation, and paragraphing, such a text as Lambarde might have left had he contemplated printing. That of the "Ephemeris" presents few problems, for it was intended only for the writer's own eyes and was therefore written in a bald and artless style and is almost without correction or alteration.

The charges Lambarde revised carefully, and the student of Elizabethan rhetoric or style would find much to interest him in a text showing all deleted words and passages, along with all additions and substitutions, indicated in some such way as they are in the quotation given above. Such a text, however, while serving a few specialists (whose needs can be meet by photography) would make more difficult a style not at best remarkable for ease of reading. In the present text, accordingly, deleted matter is ignored, and additions and alterations are silently incorporated.

The desire to provide a convenient reading text for students of social history would by itself sufficiently justify the editors in adopting an independent paragraphing, as has been done. Lambarde's own paragraphing is so unsystematic as to be impracticable for reproduction. Where he could he employed, in place of the usual paragraph indentations, lateral spaces of an inch or so between sentences. Consistently applied, this practice would be satisfactory, and the divisions of thought so marked are ordinarily such as might well be reproduced as paragraphs, but he often forgets to indicate any divisions, and his spaces vary so much as often to obscure his intention.

In modernizing the punctuation we respect not Lambarde's sense only, but his rhetoric and style as well. For some editorial discretion in the formation of sentences, he gives us good warrant by not uncommonly failing to indicate through the conventional signs the ending of one sentence and the beginning of the next.

In the standardizing of the spelling we distinguish carefully between irregular and archaic spellings, which we modernize, and archaic forms of words, which we regard as an inalienable part of Elizabethan English and for that reason retain. Clearly to be classed as forms rather than spellings are *abiden, accompt, elvish, espies* (noun), *fantasying, gaol, mo* (= more), *runagate,* and *ure.* Less readily distinguishable as forms are *harborow,* which we retain, and *auctority, bycause, practize, proining* (= pruning), and *whilest,* which we regard as lying on the other side of the dividing line and which we accordingly modernize.

For the spelling of the hundreds of names in the "Ephemeris" no simple rule is possible, and no two editors would arrive at identical results throughout. Surnames that can be said to have in our own time a standard spelling, like Butcher, Byrd, Lucas, Miller, Page, we so spell. Where among numerous variants no standard can be discerned, as with Pierce, Nichols, Willoughby, we take the names more or less as they come. Nowadays the Clarks and the Clarkes are distinct families, as are the Browns and the Brownes, the Smiths and the Smythes. In the sixteenth century these variants were spellings only, and to make a distinction between Clark and Clarke would be to risk making two men out of one, which we avoid by using one spelling. The same may be true of Cooper and Cowper, but some Elizabethans, including Lambarde, seem to make a distinction here, and in this we follow them. Unusual names, like Posyer, Hassely, and Usiner, we leave as Lambarde spells them the first time. Pelsant and Pigeon each occur a number of times in the "Ephemeris," and we somewhat arbitrarily settle on these spellings among the many that Lambarde uses. To place names we give the spellings in use today if we can identify the place named. For the few that defy recognition we keep Lambarde's spelling or modify only that of common place-name elements.

For headings of the charges we print Lambarde's own heading where he provides one (for just half the total number). When this is wanting, we take it from the endorsement, which is always present. When the data are split between heading and endorsement in the manuscript, we draw on both. Thus we preserve in the heading all data as to place, date, and occasion but avoid duplication.

Our treatment of dates in the "Ephemeris" aims at clarity and uniformity. Lambarde wrote his dates (in the margin) in every conceivable manner—in English or Latin, abbreviated or full, with Roman numerals or Arabic. We reduce all to English, with Arabic numerals. Also we change the year date between December and January, not, following Lambarde, after March 24. Lambarde's dated entries are not infrequently out of order, sometimes by as much as two or three months—probably the result of accidental omission later rectified. These dislocations we silently correct.

Of abbreviations and contractions we keep only those usual today. The same applies to numbers in the text. Losses resulting from decay or wear of the manuscripts—never more than a word or two—we indicate with angle brackets: <   >. Any words or letters standing within these brackets are the product of editorial conjecture, guided in some instances by fragments of words or letters remaining at the edges of a lacuna.

GILES E. DAWSON

Folger Library
March 9, 1961

Contents

An Ephemeris of the Certifiable Causes

of the Peace, from June, 1580 till

September, 1588, 30 Elizabethae Reginae

Introduction

AT a sale of the properties of W. G. Lambarde, Esq., of Brad-
bourne Hall, Sevenoaks, Kent, in June, 1924, the Folger Library
purchased some interesting manuscripts by William Lambarde,
the Elizabethan antiquarian.[1] These manuscripts, written in
Lambarde's own hand, consist of "An Ephemeris" and drafts of
the addresses delivered by Lambarde to quarter sessions and
special sessions in Kent for the period 1582–1601.[2]

The "Ephemeris" is apparently a memorandum book in which
William Lambarde, during the first eight years of his service as
justice of the peace in the Western Division of Kent, kept such
notes as he found it necessary or desirable to record. On the
cover of the book the title runs "An Ephemeris of the Certifiable
Causes of the Commission of the Peace from June 1580, 22 Elizabethae Reginae, till September 1588, 30 Elizabethae Reginae,"
but an examination of the contents of the book discloses the fact
that it is not confined to "certifiable causes." It includes all sorts

---

[1] Dr. Bertha Putnam has given an interesting account of other Lambarde
items in this sale but has not noted the two referred to here; see *English
Historical Review,* XLI (1926), 260–273.

[2] These addresses have not been previously published. They confirm
the fact—stated in Lambarde's diary—that Lambarde was justice of the
peace in Kent from 1580 until shortly before his death in 1601. The last
address was written for delivery at the Easter quarter sessions, 1601.

of matters which occupied Lambarde's attention, some of them matters which he dealt with alone, others matters in which he was associated with one or several other justices. It does not include any record of the general sessions of the peace. The affairs with which it deals are altogether confined to what Hasted in his *History of Kent* called the Western Division of Kent, which included the lathes of Sutton at Hone, Aylesford, and the southern part of Scray. Most of the business fell within the lathe of Aylesford, which runs north and south through the middle of the county and follows very roughly the valley of the Medway. The last entry in the book suggests that William Lambarde started another "Ephemeris" for the period following. If he did, it has disappeared.

The author, William Lambarde,[3] was a personage of such importance in the political and intellectual life of his time that it is rather amazing to discover that there is no adequate biography of him. His span of life coincided closely with that of his great mistress, Queen Elizabeth. He was born three years after her in 1536 and died two years before her in 1601. He was a Londoner, the son of John Lambarde, draper, alderman, and sheriff of London, but he spent almost all of his life in Kent and his public career was for the most part connected with Kent. Obviously he belonged to the new gentry who had made their fortunes in the city, had then acquired country estates, and by degrees had established themselves among the country families.

[3] A portrait of Lambarde in the possession of Major Gore Lambard is reproduced in *Archaeologia Cantiana*, XXXIX (1926), facing p. 131. The account of Lambarde in *Bibliotheca Topographica Britannica*, ed. John Nichols (London, 1780–90), I, 495–509, was, according to Nichols, supplied by Moulton Lambard, a lineal descendant of William Lambarde. Lambarde's family connections he recorded himself in his diary, preserved among the Lambarde manuscripts and published in *Miscellanea Genealogica et Heraldica*, II (1876), 99 ff. Lambarde seems to have begun this diary in 1587. At his death it passed with his estate to his heirs and was continued by his successors until 1798. It contains almost nothing about Lambarde's public life.

Introduction

Of William Lambarde's education we know nothing before his admission to Lincoln's Inn in 1556.[4] In view of his scholarly attainments it is hard to believe that he was not a university man, but there is no record of him either at Oxford or Cambridge. His mother died when he was four years old, and some time afterward his father took a second wife, who survived him.[5] Probably William resided with his father and his stepmother in London until his father died in 1554. He entered Lincoln's Inn two years later. What happened to him during the years immediately following is pure speculation. He inherited from his father the manor of Westcombe in East Greenwich [6] and may have resided there off and on until his first marriage, with Jane Moulton, in 1570.[7] Evidently he then took up his residence at the home of his father-in-law, George Moulton, at St. Clere's, Ightham, Kent. Jane Lambarde died in 1573, but apparently William continued to reside at Ightham until shortly before his second marriage in 1583, when he removed to Halling, probably to the episcopal palace there, the lease of which his second wife had inherited from her father.[8] He was still living in Halling in 1597, although his second wife had died ten years earlier. During the first three years of

[4] *The Dictionary of National Biography* gives the date as February 9. Lambarde in his diary says February 6.

[5] The last will of this stepmother is printed in *Archaeologia Cantiana,* V (1863), 252–253. She was apparently on good terms with William and bequeathed him £10.

[6] This manor was purchased by his father in 1544, according to Lambarde's diary. It remained in the family until 1649.

[7] Lambarde, in his dedicatory letter transmitting the manuscript of his *Perambulation of Kent,* dates the letter at St. Clere's, January 31, 1570/71. His first wife was born in 1553 and was therefore seventeen years his junior. His second wife was born the following year. She was the daughter of Robert Dene of Halling and the widow of W. Dallison, who was apparently the son of the justice of the same name, not the justice himself as Dr. Putnam says in her *Early Treatises on the Practice of the Justices of the Peace* (Oxford, 1924), p. 111, n. 1.

[8] In the past it had occasionally been the residence of Bishop John Fisher, the Roman Catholic martyr.

the period covered by the "Ephemeris," Lambarde, then, was residing at Ightham, during the last five at Halling, both of them in the lathe of Aylesford, less than ten miles apart as the crow flies.

It was characteristic of Lambarde that wherever his interest lay his pen followed fast. When he was a student in Lincoln's Inn he fell under the spell of Laurence Nowell, a diligent antiquarian, learned in Anglo-Saxon. At his instigation Lambarde published, in 1568, a collection and Latin translation of the laws of the Anglo-Saxons (*Archaionomia*), the first of its kind.[9] Dr. Lieberman, the editor of the standard modern edition of these laws, observed of Lambarde's work that as "a pioneer in an unknown land" his work was good.[10] Lambarde retained his interest in Anglo-Saxon to the end, sometimes revealing it in odd ways, as when he signed his name in Anglo-Saxon letters and printed an Anglo-Saxon alphabet in the introduction to his second book, *A Perambulation of Kent*.

This second book was also a pioneer in its field, the first of the county histories. Lambarde evidently regarded it as an installment of a more comprehensive study,[11] an enterprise which he abandoned when he learned that William Camden was at work on his *Britannia*. Camden himself acknowledged that virtually

[9] Lambarde refers to Nowell in his diary as *"Mei amantissimi."* It is not quite clear whether this collection was mainly the work of Nowell or Lambarde. Strype says that Nowell went abroad and left the manuscript in Lambarde's hand for publication. Lambarde in his diary says that Nowell went to France in 1567, the same year probably that *Archaionomia* went to press.

[10] Quoted by Sir William Holdsworth, *History of English Law* (London, 1924), V, 403.

[11] This fact appears in his letter dedicating the *Perambulation of Kent* to Thomas Wotton. Lambarde notes in his diary that the book was printed March 12, 1575/76, but it actually did not appear until a little later. The manuscript of the book was sold to Maggs Bros. at the Hodgson sale (1924) and subsequently passed into the possession of the Kent Archaeological Society (*Archaeologia Cantiana*, XXXVIII [1926], 90 n.).

all he had to say about Kent was taken from Lambarde, "a man right well endowed with excellent learning." [12] And yet one can wish that Lambarde had told us more about Kent as he knew it at first hand, rather than as he had read about it in ancient authors. In any case, we are lucky that he saw fit to write about Kent, and we are luckier still that when he became J.P. in Kent his pen followed him once more in producing *Eirenarcha*, the best sixteenth-century handbook for justices of the peace. Here was a man holding office in Kent who has provided us both with an account of his county and a classical account of his office in the county.

Actually Lambarde's appointment to office, if we are to take him at his word, provoked him to write his *Eirenarcha*,[13] the first edition of which appeared about two and a half years after he had been "put" in the commission of peace. He revised the book for the second edition, published in 1588. Subsequent editions show relatively little variation from the 1588 edition. An appendix of documents and an elaborate index were added in the second edition, but the most striking change was a breakdown of the text from two books in the first edition to four books in the second.[14] It is on the whole surprising that after eight years in office Lambarde found so little need for change in the contents of his treatise. The changes in form were designed to make the book more readily usable. It is, and was intended to be, a practical working handbook of justice. All the illustrative documents, writs,

[12] *Britain,* tr. Philemon Holland (London, 1610), p. 323.

[13] See his letter dedicatory to Lord Chancellor Bromley in the first edition of *Eirenarcha,* reproduced by Putnam, *English Historical Review,* XLI (1926), 263.

[14] The various editions are set forth in the *Short-Title Catalogue.* There seem to have been three variations of the first edition, one bearing the imprint 1581, the other two 1582. Seven other editions appeared by 1610. A "module" or preliminary outline of the book in manuscript was sold at the Hodgson sale and is now in B.M. Add. MS 41137. A dispute between publishers over publication rights in 1594 is recorded in *Acta Cancellaria,* ed. Cecil Monro (London, 1847), pp. 649–650.

Introduction

bonds, and the like, are drawn from Kent, and Lambarde did not hesitate to use his own name or the names of his fellow justices in the text. He was even careful in later editions to substitute new names for old as new justices replaced the old ones. The frequent use of the name of his father-in-law, George Moulton, in the first edition of the book, substantiates what will be apparent in the "Ephemeris": that he and Moulton were very closely associated in their official work.[15]

The most obscure part of Lambarde's official life is his parliamentary career. He probably sat in the House of Commons in 1563–1566 for Aldborough, Yorkshire, and he probably wrote the only reasonably full account of parliamentary procedure which has survived from the sixteenth century. And yet Lambarde's name appears only once in the *Journals* of the House of Commons and never on committees in which Kentish affairs were involved. He probably owed his seat in 1563 to government influence, and he must certainly have been regarded as a government man. We must conclude that he had some facility as a speaker in view of the fact that he was selected year after year to deliver the annual charge to the grand jury at the Kent quarter sessions. The one mention of his activities in the House of Commons is in the second session of the Parliament of 1563 on November 8, 1566.[16] On that occasion, apparently, Lambarde

[15] Lambarde named his first son Moulton *"in gratia soceris mei amantissimi Georgii Multoni"* (*Diary*).

[16] *Journals of All the Parliaments . . . of Queen Elizabeth*, ed. Sir Simonds D'Ewes (London, 1682), p. 128. A manuscript copy of Lambarde's treatise on procedure is preserved in B.M. Add. MS 5123. Professor John E. Neale has made considerable use of it in his book, *The Elizabethan House of Commons* (London, [1949]). It was not published until 1641 and was reprinted in *Harleian Miscellany* (1808–11), IV, 559–571. Professor Neale informs me that the printed version reveals some seventeenth-century additions to the text. He has found no copy of the manuscript in Lambarde's hand. In Neale's judgment Lambarde probably wrote his treatise in 1587. Neale agrees with me that the evidence of Lambarde's presence in the House of Commons in 1586/87 is not sufficient to justify

8

delivered himself at length on the thorny question of the succession, a strange performance for a government man, since the Queen was strongly opposed to any discussion of the question. It is quite conceivable that in consequence Lambarde fell into disfavor in Court and that his parliamentary career abruptly terminated. Certainly he was high in government favor later, but it is still, I think, very doubtful whether he ever sat in the House again, though it is a little hard to reconcile his notes on procedure with that view of the matter. There is a strong presumption that the notes were written in 1587. Certainly there are parts of them that could not have been written earlier. But in view of entries in the "Ephemeris" during the periods when the Parliament of 1586–1587 was sitting (October 29–December 2, and February 15–March 23), it does not seem possible that Lambarde attended its sessions.

The last important work from Lambarde's pen lies beyond the scope of the "Ephemeris." It is his *Archion,* which bears the subtitle *A Commentary upon the High Courts of Justice in England.* It was dedicated to Sir Robert Cecil in a letter dated Lincoln's Inn, October 22, 1591. By Lambarde's own account he had been writing it off and on for many years. It was not published until 1635. A good deal of it is historical in character and has to do with the origins of the courts. Lambarde's findings in these particulars would no longer be regarded as sound. Probably the most valuable part of the book is his account of the Star Chamber, easily the best sixteenth-century account of that court. Lambarde treated his whole subject rather as an advocate than as a historian. Throughout he argued strongly for the chancery and the prerogative courts, an attitude, for a judge of the common law, in marked contrast to that of the common lawyer in the next reign. Certainly there is nothing in what he wrote to anticipate the issues over these matters which arose later. Indeed,

---

the positive assertion of that fact in *The Elizabethan House of Commons,* p. 363.

with the exception of his outburst in the House of Commons in 1566, there is nothing in what he wrote or in what he did to indicate that he was any other than a loyal supporter of Elizabeth's policy both in state and in church. But there is no sound reason to believe that he ever participated actively in matters of statecraft. A letter which he is said to have written to Burghley in July, 1585, urging active English intervention in the Low Countries, is almost certainly from someone else much more intimately connected with the government and much more closely associated with the Queen.[17]

Lambarde's connection with Lincoln's Inn (the foremost of the Inns of Chancery, where he was made bencher in 1579) and his account of the Court of Chancery as set forth in *Archion* in 1591 indicate an interest in and an expert knowledge of the subject which probably account for his appointment as Master of Chancery in June of the following year. Reports of the Masters during his term of office reveal the fact that he was active in the business of the court.[18] Sometime or other Lambarde made a collection of reports of cases in chancery which were later used by George Carew (or Carey) in his *Report on Causes in Chancery* (1650).[19] He evidently spent some part of his time during the last decade of his life at Lincoln's Inn. Nevertheless, he continued to serve as justice of the peace in Kent until his death, although unfortunately we have no second "Ephemeris" from

[17] The letter is printed in John Nichols, *Progresses . . . of Queen Elizabeth* (London, 1823), III, 554. Its reference to a conference with the secret agent of Henry of Navarre and to various conferences with the Queen indicate a personality much closer to the inward workings of the government than Lambarde apparently ever was.

[18] *Acta Cancellaria* reports four cases in which Lambarde was involved, falling between the dates December 4, 1595 and July 15, 1600. Lambarde was an associate, by the way, of Sir John Tyndal, the same Tyndal who was assassinated later by a disappointed litigant; he named Tyndal one of the overseers of his will (Holdsworth, *op. cit.*, V, 259, n. 9; *Archaeologia Cantiana*, V [1863], 253).

[19] Holdsworth, *op. cit.*, V, 277.

which to judge how active he was. We do have the manuscripts of his annual speeches to the grand jury at quarter sessions in Kent up to the very year of his death.

Lambarde was probably primarily a student of laws. He was also active in the administration of the laws: of the common law in Kent, of equity as Master of Chancery. He evidently had a genius for friendship. Wherever he was he gathered close friends about him. Two of his sons were named after his associates in the Kent quarter sessions. Another of these associates, Lord Cobham, he called his "father-like good Lord." [20] He asked the wives of two other associates to keep watch over the education of his daughter. He named one of his associate Masters of Chancery as an overseer of his will. Lord Burghley was his friend and patron, William Camden one of his admirers. Sir Julius Caesar described him as "a deep and learned scholar, a great common lawyer, and a religious, conscionable, and worthy gentleman." [21] Even John Stow, the London tailor-historian, referred to him as his "loving friend." [22] One gathers the impression that he was a modest man, very learned in the law, widely known, and very warmly regarded by those with whom he worked.

Only one conference between him and Elizabeth is recorded. It took place at East Greenwich in 1601 about a fortnight before his death and was occasioned by Lambarde's presentation to the Queen of his report on the public records in the Tower.[23] She raised some question about them, her mind evidently still full of the Essex treason with all its personal and political implica-

[20] Nichols, *op. cit.*, III, 558. Lambarde's will is printed in *Archaeologia Cantiana*, V (1863), 253–256.

[21] *Acta Cancellaria*, 15 n.

[22] John Stow, *Survey of London*, ed. Charles L. Kingsford (Oxford, 1908), II, 253.

[23] He was made Keeper of the Records of the Rolls Chapel by Sir Thomas Egerton on May 26, 1597 and Keeper of the Records of the Tower on January 21, 1601. But apart from the passage above we have no record of his activities in these connections.

tions. "In those days," she said, "force and arms did prevail, but now the wit of foxes is everywhere on foot, so that hardly a faithful or virtuous man may be found." And then she thanked Lambarde for his pains, clasped his report to her bosom, and went away to her prayers. "Farewell," she said, "good and honest Lambarde." In the last days of his life he recorded the interview.[24] Whether he so intended it or not, it was an appropriate *nunc dimittis.*

Lambarde's "Ephemeris" contains very little about his personal life which we do not get from other sources. It is valuable for his official life in Kent, but it is obviously nothing like a complete record. The days accounted for over a period of about nine years are about two hundred. In only one year do the days accounted for exceed thirty, and the average is about twenty-two per annum. In some years there are no entries for months at a time. For example, there are no entries from April 3, 1581, to July 8, 1581; only one between September and December, 1583. For the most part Lambarde's activities as disclosed in the "Ephemeris" have to do with the taking of recognizances for keeping the peace and the certifying of them at quarter sessions, the licensing of alehouses, the punishment of bastardy and provision for the support of bastards, and thievery. It is surprising to discover that there is only one doubtful instance of a case arising under the Statute of Apprentices, none at all of one arising under the laws against priests and recusants. Strype's assumption that Lambarde's personal difficulties were caused in part by his persistent "search after such as were disaffected persons, priests and others," has no support at all in this memorandum book.[25] There is very little evidence of civil disorder and, curiously enough, in the very month when the Spanish Armada was in the Channel, nothing at all about it and no evident preparations for resisting invasion. We certainly cannot conclude that Lambarde was not

[24] Nichols, *op. cit.*, III, 552.

[25] John Strype, *Annals of the Reformation* (London, 1725–31), III, 493.

engaged in such matters, particularly in Kent, which would almost certainly have felt the first shock of invasion had the Spaniards triumphed in the Channel fight. All of which means that we must accept the "Ephemeris" simply for what it contains and make no assumptions about what it does not contain.

There are interesting notes by the way which we wish were more complete than they are. We learn, for example, that Lambarde assisted in the taking of the musters in Kent in 1580, even before he was formally sworn into office. We learn that he served on the commission of sewers of the Medway, an important job which involved virtual control of inland waterways. We learn that he was the author of the accepted plan for the Kent House of Correction. The plan itself is still to be found among his papers.[26] There are some interesting references to the imposition of local assessments for the repair of bridges, for the building of gaols, and for the relief of the poor.[27] There is some evidence of friction between the royal purveyors and the local constables. There is a good deal about rogues and vagabonds and "Egyptians," and one case in which two wandering minstrels were sent to gaol for six days. There is something about poaching. There is at least one case about a man refusing to work upon the highways and one apparently covering a breach in a wage contract. There is only one reference to the levy of soldiers and the equipment of them.

The procedure followed in different sorts of cases can almost always be found clearly stated in Lambarde's *Eirenarcha*. I think it sufficient in this connection to cite the pertinent passages in *Eirenarcha* as the text seems to call for them. My references are to the 1610 edition of that work.

Conyers Read

[26] B.M. Add. MS 41137, ff. 175–179.
[27] There is some material in Lambarde's hand on gaol money in B.M. Add. MS 41137, ff. 180–190. I have not been able to examine it.

An Ephemeris of the Certifiable Causes

of the Peace, from June, 1580 till

September, 1588, 30 Elizabethae Reginae

1580

April–May I was put in the commission of the peace 6 August 1579 et 21 Elizabethae Reginae, and I took the oath 3 June 1580 and 22 Elizabethae Reginae, and between these days I assisted Sir Christopher Alleyn, Sir Thomas Cotton, and Mr. Robert Byng in taking the musters at Shorne the 25 April and at Frindsbury the 26 April for the Lord Cobham's division. And likewise I assisted the justices of the other three divisions of the lathe of Aylesford in taking their musters at Malling, Tonbridge, and Borough Green, because the commission of the musters was a general commission by itself, etc.[28]

June–July The last of June 1580 and the first of July I joined with my father-in-law, George Moulton, in the examination of Baptiste Bristow, Edward Rootes, John Romyne, Thomas Brissenden, and Nicholas Miller concerning a robbery done upon

---

[28] For figures on this muster, see E. E. Rich, *Economic History Review,* 2nd ser., II (1950), 254.

the said Baptiste, etc., by virtue of letters from the lords of the Privy Council.

The 9 of July I assisted Mr. Willughby and Mr. Potter in the examination of Oliver Booby of Chipstead, by virtue of the said letters. All which examinations I have delivered to the Lord Chief Baron, upon his request of the same by his letters.

August   The 26 August, being at Tonbridge in the execution of the commission of sewers for Medway, Sir Thomas Fane, Sir Christopher Alleyn, and I sent Thomas Chambers, William Cosin, and Thomas Norham of Tonbridge to the gaol for keeping ale-houses obstinately and against the commandment of sundry justices which had put them down.

September   The 20 of September my father-in-law and I examined John Sone, by virtue of the said letters from the lords, and bound him to appear at the quarter sessions at Maidstone. The same day he and I sent Walter Pelsant of Borough Green to the gaol for keeping an alehouse there obstinately against the commandment of Mr. Byng and Mr. Richers.

The same day also he and I bound Sylvester Swan of Ightham to the peace against John Bound the younger of Ightham, tailor, the said Walter Pelsant and Edward Rootes of Ightham, shoemaker, being his sureties; but this was released.[29]

The 26 of September Sir Thomas Fane and I took sureties of Thomas Chambers aforesaid, namely, Thomas Codd of Tonbridge, innholder, and William Lucas of the same, shoemaker; and likewise we took bond with the said William Cosin, William Atmer of Penshurst, yeoman, and John Cosin of Tonbridge, tailor, and with Thomas Norham, Isaac Fray of Hadlow, husbandman, and Nicholas Dynes of Tonbridge, laborer, the principals in 10 *li.* the piece and the sureties in 5 *li.* the piece, with

[29] This whole matter of sureties to keep the peace is discussed in *Eirenarcha* (1610 ed.), pp. 75 ff.

condition that the principals shall no more keep alehouses, etc.

The 27 and 28 September the Lord Cobham and I licensed James Hawkes, Thomas Pigeon, and George Colt, all of Chalk, to keep alehouses in their then dwelling houses there, and we took the said Hawkes bound in 10 *li.*, Andrew Smith of Higham and Reignold Hawkes of <Shorne>, his sureties, bound in 5 *li.* apiece, with the usual condition <which I> have devised for that purpose. Colt and Phig<eon   .> [30]

My father and I joined in certifying our knowledge to the bishop concerning the good behavior of Margaret Tebold to be married, etc. Likewise bound, and with them, William Page of Shorne, gentleman, and Stephen Colt of the same, yeoman, as sureties in the like sums and under the like conditions.

The said Lord and I bound Richard Williams of Higham, yeoman, in 100 marks, to his good behavior, but that was released, etc.

October   The 3 of October my father-in-law and I bound Walter Pelsant aforesaid from keeping an alehouse any more; his sureties were Reignold Pelsant and Nicholas Miller of Wrotham, yeomen.

The 4 October I certified at the quarter sessions [31] the said recognizances of Walter Pelsant, Thomas Chambers, William Cosin, and Thomas Norham for not keeping alehouses, and the said recognizances of James Hawkes, Thomas Pigeon, and George Colt for the keeping of good rule in their alehouses, and the said recognizance of John Sone for his appearance aforesaid, the said Walter Pelsant and John Usiner of Wrotham, butchers, being his sureties, which recognizance was then forfeit by his default of appearance.

The 25 October I delivered to the Lord Chief Baron the said examination of John Sone aforesaid.

[30] On the licensing of alehouses, cf. *ibid.*, pp. 353–354.
[31] Cf. *ibid.*, p. 103.

My father-in-law and I entreated Nordashe of Kemsing to give over aleselling because no alehouse had been kept there within the memory of any man.

November The 25 of November I and my father-in-law took order for the punishment of Joan Pitchford of Seal, widow, and Alice Hylles of the same town, for the bearing of two bastards,[32] and for the punishment of Thomas Byrd of the said town, turner, and Thomas Pigeon, late of the same town, turner, the reputed fathers of the said bastards, and according to that order the said Thomas and Alice were set in a cart at Sevenoaks the next day and the said Joan scourged at the same cart's tail there; as for Pigeon, he was fled long before. We then also took two obligations for the relief of the parish and for the keeping of those bastards. All which appeareth in the order and obligations aforesaid.

The 29 November my father-in-law and I took order for the punishment of John Manser, alias Butcher, late of Seal, and Joan Pierse of the same, for the begetting and bearing of a bastard maid child, according to which order the said Joan was scourged at Seal the said day; as for John, he was fled before. We then also took an obligation of her for the keeping of that bastard, etc.

The same day we wrote our letters to Sir Thomas Walsingham for the staying of Mr. Reignold Peckham, who was arrested and brought to him by the name of Thomas Clark.

The 30 of November I joined with Sir Thomas Walsingham in sending Reignold Peckham abovenamed to the Lord Chief Baron to London, who was apprehended in the watch at Foots Cray about ten of the clock in the morning upon the Monday before; the parts of this doing appeareth in my papers of notes thereof.

[32] The procedure here follows that prescribed in a statute of 1575/76 (18 Eliz., cap. 3). See *Statutes of the Realm* (London, 1810–22), IV, pt. 1, 610.

[*December?*] The fifth day I served under the Lord Cobham in some small < of the> peace, whereof there is no record, etc. I sent 11 December to the Lord Chief Baron by my cousin Wale, at his lordship's request, another copy of the examinations concerning Baptiste Bristow's robbery.

On Christmas day my father-in-law and I did send Robert Baker of Kemsing to the gaol, upon his confession of the felonious taking of nineteen sheep, and took a recognizance of 20 *li.* of Richard Kipps of Kemsing to give in evidence, etc., at the next gaol delivery.

1581

January The said John Manser, being apprehended, was brought to my father-in-law and me and sent to be whipped, according to our said order, at Seal, 4 January.[33]

John Crook of Edenbridge and Thomas Andrews of Kemsing were bound by us to give evidence, etc., against the said Robert Baker, 23 January.

John Wood of Westminster, waterman, was by us committed to the gaol for robbing Henry Blower of Southwark, wax chandler, on Gad's Hill, and the said Blower bound to give evidence, etc., 23 January.

February The 27 February, at the assizes at Rochester, I certified the causes of Saxey aforesaid, Baker aforesaid, and Wood aforesaid, and the cause of one Walter, a runagate physician, in which I had assisted Sir Thomas Fane at Tonbridge.

March The 23 of March my father-in-law and I took two obligations, the one of John Hylles and William Hylles of Seal, and the other of Margaret Denne, for the keeping of a bastard be-

[33] See November 29 above.

gotten by the said William on her and born at Seal. We took no order for the punishment because of the general pardon looked for, etc.

3 April My father-in-law and I took the examination of John Gladwell, charged with the felonious taking of wheat and peas, and the information of Reignold Hawkes, and [blank] Innifer, concerning the same, and bailed the said Gladwell under his bond of 20 *li.* and the bond of 10 *li.* of John Burges. This examination, with the information and recognizances, I certified at Rochester, 3 July.

8 July My father-in-law and I made a warrant against the constable of Town Malling, William Bennet, and his wife, for the arresting of Joan Darrell of felony and not bringing her to any justice of peace, etc.

19 July I bound Thomas Weston of Ightham, in 40 *li.*, and his father, William Weston (as his manucaptor [34]), in 20 *li.*, to keep the peace against Wombwell Bound of Ightham. And then also I bound the said Wombwell, in 40 *li.*, and Richard Cornford (as his manucaptor), in 20 *li.*, to keep the peace against the said Thomas Weston; which recognizance I took of discretion [35] for that they had fought together and neither of them would pray the peace against the other.

25 July The 25 July I bound George Pelsant of Ightham, in 40 *li.*, and his father (as mainpernor), William Pelsant, in 20 *li.*, to keep the peace against Thomas Weston, etc.

The 26 July I joined with my father, Mr. Richers, etc., in war-

[34] Acting as manucaptor or mainpernor (see below) is the same as putting up bail for a prisoner. Lambarde discusses this in *Eirenarcha*, pp. 340–341.

[35] On this matter of discretion, see *Eirenarcha*, p. 77.

20

rants to understand the number of the alehouses in our end of the limit.[36]

Ultimo July   My father-in-law and I bound James Franklin, in 20 *li.*, and Stephen Mylles and Edward Rootes, in 5 *li.* each of them, all being of Ightham, shoemakers, for the good abearing [37] of the said James and for his appearance at the next quarter sessions, etc.

August   Sir Thomas Cotton, Sir Christopher Alleyn, Thomas Willughby, Robert Richers, and I sat at Borough Green for the allowance and disallowance of alehouses, where we took bond of Roger Meare of Mereworth, tippler, for keeping good order in his alehouse, he being bound in 10 *li.* and John Betts and William Ramkyn of Mereworth aforesaid, his sureties, each in 5 *li.*

There we agreed upon an assess of 12 *li.* 15 *s.* to be levied in our division for the reparation of Hockenbury bridge. And within a few days after we made precepts for the said sum and for the putting down of the alehouses which we had disallowed.

23 August   Sir Christopher Alleyn, my father-in-law, and I joined in the examination of eight persons that counterfeited their apparel and language as the rogues called Egyptians were wont to do, and we sent them to the gaol.

26 September   At the quarter sessions, 26 September 1581, holden at Maidstone, I certified the said recognizances of Meare and George Pelsant; the other of Weston, Bound, and Franklin I released and so certified them there also.

10 October   My father-in-law and I took the examination of William Greaves of Gravesend, arrested for suspicion of the felony of thirty sheep, and the informations of Simon Gray, Richard

[36] The meaning here is obscure.
[37] On good abearing, see *Eirenarcha,* p. 115.

Clipsam, and Robert Cole concerning the same, and committed the prisoner and bound Gray and Cole to give in evidence, viz., either of them in 20 *li.*

28 October   Mr. Byng and I bound Henry Swan of Chalk to the peace against Mr. Hull and Adrian Walker, his tenant, in 20 *li.*, with his brother, John Swan, in 10 *li.*

The same time we sent John Hogben to the gaol for conveying ten pounds in a purse from Thomas Morgan, the information and examination whereof I left with Mr. Byng.

Reignolds of Ightham was by my father-in-law bound to his good behavior; he was afterward executed for a burglary.

9 November   My father-in-law and I sent John Horsley to the gaol for stealing a bolster and sheet from Thomas Wright of Gravesend, and bound the said Wright, in 10 *li.*, to give in evidence, etc.

December   The 5 of December I committed Isaac Carr to the gaol for stealing nine sheep, and I bound Thomas Curtis, Thomas Fisher, and John Bote to give evidence, in 5 *li.* every of them.

The second December I made a precept of the peace [38] for Thomas Gatford of Higham against Thomas Newman of the same town, laborer, and the 14 December I bound him, in 20 *li.*, and John Goody and John Woodgreen of Higham, yeomen, each in 10 *li.*, for the peace and appearance, etc.

16 December   My father-in-law and I bailed Andrew B<rewer> of Seal, being charged with the burglary committed in the house of Alice Fuller of Ightham, widow. He was bound, in 40 *li.*, and Richard Brantfield and Robert Hunt of Ightham, yeomen, in 20 *li.* apiece.

[38] See *Eirenarcha*, p. 85.

22

An Ephemeris

1582

January The 2 of January I likewise bound the said [39] Thomas Gatford, in 20 *li.*, and Mr. Thomas Cobham of Higham, in 20 *li.*, as his surety, for the peace and appearance, etc., at the suit of the said Newman.

The 3 of January I sent to the gaol Richard Hanwood, butcher, for stealing 24 *li.* 5 *s.* in money from William Latham, his master, and bound the said William to sue, etc., and to bring Thomas Cockes or Robert Latham with him, who were at the apprehension. Remember to send for Christopher Bowle, the borsholder [40] of Milton, who arrested him and told the money.

15 March These examinations, informations, and recognizances concerning William Greaves, John Hogben, John Horsley, Isaac Carr, Richard Hanwood, and Andrew Brewer I certified at the assizes at Rochester, 15 March 1581 [1582].[41]

1 April My father-in-law and I bound John Swan of Wrotham to the good behavior, to be kept till Easter 1584, in 20 *li.*, for whom William Lever and Henry Lever of Wrotham, yeomen, did understake, in 10 *li.* every of them.

4 April My father-in-law and I sent Richard West of Ightham and Agnes Payne to the gaol for not finding sureties of the good behavior.

8 April My father-in-law and I sent to the gaol William Barra for getting Elizabeth [blank], servant to William Clark, alias

---

[39] At this point on the margin Lambarde has written "look after."

[40] On this office, see Lambarde, *The Duties of Constables, Borsholders, Tithingmen, and . . . Other . . . Ministers of the Peace* (1610 ed.), pp. 6 ff.

[41] The previous entry concerning Brewer, dated December 16, immediately precedes this one in the MS.

Butcher, of Northfleet, tippler, with child and refusing to give sureties of his good behavior.

12 April I and my father-in-law delivered out of the gaol Nicholas Byford of Gravesend, tippler, whom my Lord Cobham and I sent to the gaol for keeping an alehouse against prohibition, taking him bound in 10 *li.*, and Randal Jones of Gravesend, waterman, and Miles Hudson of Milton, laborer, his sureties, in 5 *li.* the piece, for not keeping from henceforth, etc.

16 April I bound Thomas Taylor the younger of Meopham, yeoman, in 10 *li.*, and his sureties, John Child and Robert Averell of the same town, husbandmen, in 5 *li.* the piece, for keeping the peace towards Thomas Wilson of Meopham, laborer.

24 April I certified at the quarter sessions at Maidstone all the recognizances aforesaid that are to be sent thither, and there was the fine of 20 *s.* set upon Nicholas Byford aforesaid.

7 June Mr. Byng, Mr. Somer, and I took bond of the wives of two Coles of Gravesend for their appearance at the next gaol delivery for the hurt of [blank] Sacher.

9 June I bound John Alkin of Horton, vicar, in 20 *li.*, to keep the peace against Walter Heming of Dartford, yeoman, and his two sureties, William Steer of Wrotham, vicar, and Nicholas Miller of the same, yeoman, in 10 *li.* each of them, I promising to save Nicholas Miller harmless.

My father-in-law and I bailed Elizabeth Johnson of Kemsing, widow, till the next gaol delivery, binding her, in 40 *li.*, and Samuel Walmesley of Shipbourne, butcher, in 20 *li.*, and Robert Hunt of Ightham, yeoman, in 20 *li.* as her sureties.

14 June I and others held a special gaol delivery at Maidstone for the rogues, at which we adjudged seven and punished them, etc.

16 July My father-in-law and I bound Richard Cowper of Tonbridge, laborer, and William Children of the same, gentleman, in 20 *li.* the piece, for the good behavior and appearance of the said Richard at Easter sessions of the peace next to come, upon the suspicion of getting Susan Waters of Tonbridge with child. Remember to send for Andrew Turk and to bind him also for the like suspicion.

My father-in-law and I did, some days before, send to the gaol Nicholas Swan for small pickeries, and bound Nicholas Hassely, to give evidence, in 5 *li.*

I examined William Posyer (being in the gaol) upon the stealing of a horse of one [blank] Chandler of Ashurst, and I bound the said Chandler and John Rolfe of Seal, smith, to give evidence, either in 10 *li.*

I wrote to my Lord of Dover in commendation of Simon Haxup, schoolmaster at Knole, to be admitted into the ministry of the church.

19 July I certified to the assizes at Maidstone these causes of Coles's wives, Elizabeth Johnson, Nicholas Swan, and William Posyer, with the informations, examinations, and recognizances thereto belonging. And I have remaining with me the information against Robert Gilman, etc.

24 July My father-in-law and I bound Robert Hylles of Everham, to his good behavior and to appear at the next quarter sessions, in 40 *li.*, and his pledges, William Hylles of Everham and Richard Pickerel of the same, in 20 *li.* apiece.

31 July   Master Roger Twysden and I sent to the gaol John and Robert Gates for breaking the house and taking away 26 *s.* of Joan Gates of Wateringbury, whom we bound, in 10 *li.*, to give evidence.

2 August   Sir Christopher Alleyn and I sent to the gaol John Sheer for stealing six silver spoons, and bound Edmund Ware to give evidence.

25 September   I certified to the quarter sessions at Maidstone the recognizances of John Alkin, Robert Hylles, and Richard Cowper, which Cowper is to be called at Easter sessions.

The same day Mr. Thomas Randolph and I bound Richard Reader of Boughton Monchelsea, yeoman, in 100 *li.*, for his good behavior, and Richard Wood of Chart, yeoman, his surety, in 50 *li.* We then also bound Walter Reader of Boughton aforesaid, yeoman, in 100 *li.*, for his good behavior, and the said Richard Reader, his surety, in 50 *li.* And these are to appear at the Easter sessions unless we shall in the meanwhile release them.

2 October   Mr. Richers and I joined in the examination and bailment of George Pelsant, charged with the stealing of a sheep, binding him, in 40 *li.*, and his father, William Pelsant, in 20 *li.*, and George Hawkes (all of Ightham), in 20 *li.*, for his appearance at the next gaol delivery.

18 October   Mr. Rudstone, Mr. Thomas Fane, Mr. Fludd, and I joined in the examination and committing to gaol of Thomas Ward, Bartholomew Martin (or Taylor), and Halley, apprehended upon suspicion of felony. These examinations remain with Mr. Thomas Fane.

The same time I joined with the said persons in committing to the gaol Thomas Wollet of New Hythe, charged with a rape.

6 November   My father-in-law and I joined in a certificate for Elizabeth Canow of Hartley to be married to John Milles, vicar of Rodmersham.

3 December   My father-in-law and I joined with Sir Christopher Alleyn, Mr. Willughby, Mr. Byng, and Mr. Richers in certifying the birth and behavior of Richard Pierson of Ightham for his safe passage and recovery of lands in Westmorland.

5 December   The Lord Cobham, Sir Christopher Alleyn, and I took the information of John Arnold of Maidstone against Robert Gilman, etc., for the taking of a cloth, etc., feloniously, and bound him, in 20 *li.*, to give in evidence.

11 December   My father-in-law and I took order for a bastard child born by Susan Waters at Hildenborough and begotten by Richard Cowper there, as we thought, and took bond of her for 6 *d.* by week, etc. Send for <   >hyrst, the constable.

1583

Remember to renew at the Easter sessions the Register of the Poor at Ightham.

16 January   My father-in-law and I assisted Sir Christopher Alleyn in taking bond for the peace against all men of William Petley of Ightham, in 10 *li.*, and of George Hawkes, his surety, in 5 *li.*; and likewise of George Hawkes, in 10 *li.*, and the said William Petley, his surety, in 5 *li.*, and to appear at the next quarter sessions after Easter. It was forthwith released.

23 February   Sir Christopher Alleyn and I examined sundry persons at Sevenoaks concerning the suspicion of willful poisoning of William Brightrede by Thomas Heyward and Parnel, his now wife, then wife of the said William.

27 February Sir Christopher Alleyn, Mr. Thomas Fane, Mr. Twysden, Mr. Richers, and I sat at Town Malling to inquire of a riot and affrays between Mr. George Catlin and his men and the servants of Mr. Bonham.

28 February Sir Christopher Alleyn, Mr. John Lennard, and I examined divers other persons concerning the said William Brightrede's death and concerning the like suspicion of poisoning of Joan, late wife of the said Heyward. And we then committed the said Heyward and Parnel to the gaol.

4 March At the assizes at Rochester, 4 March, 25 Elizabeth, I certified the examinations aforesaid with two sundry recognizances concerning the same. And there also we all of the commission of the peace agreed upon a draft for the house of correction which I had penned,[42] and we also wrote in the behalf of a constable that was arrested by the Knight Marshal's men at the complaint of a purveyor.

7 April At the quarter sessions at Maidstone after Easter I certified the recognizances for [the] Readers. I then also renewed the Register Book for the Poor at Ightham.

10 April I am to certify at the gaol delivery the examinations of Elizabeth Leighton, taken for felony before my Lord Cobham, and to change the bond of those that should give evidence against her, which also is done.

From my coming to Halling, 15 May 1583.[43]

17 May William Gilman the younger was apprehended and brought before me, whom, for not being able to give surety of

[42] This may be the document from Lambarde's papers now in B.M. Add. MS 41137, ff. 175–179.

[43] Probably the date of Lambarde's removal from Ightham to Halling, shortly before his second marriage.

his good abearing, I sent to Maidstone gaol. He is also indicted of felony and I have changed the warrant.

21 May There was holden at Maidstone a special session of the peace for the rogues, where divers were bound and whipped.

I have signed a license for Thomas Godfrey to beg till Allhallontide (for his house burnt) within the limits of the Lord Cobham only.

23 June I bound Francis Whitepaine of Yalding, yeoman, to the peace against Richard Acton of Yalding, clothier, with four manucaptors, by force of a supplicavit out of the Chancery.[44]

13 July At Cobham Hall my Lord and I licensed Edward Doret of Cobham to keep an alehouse. He was bound, in 20 *li.*, and Thomas Harris and William Waite of Cobham, in 10 *li.* either of them, as his sureties, with the common condition.

The same day we wrote to such of other parishes as occupied lands in Allhallows to contribute after the rate of 2 *d.* in the pound of their said lands towards the relief of the poor of Allhallows.

15 July I certified the examinations and recognizances at the assizes at Maidstone which were to be certified thither.

18 July By direction from Sir Thomas Gawdy, Justice of Assizes, I wrote to Mr. Taylor, vicar of Sevenoaks, etc.

20 July At Cobham Hall my Lord, Sir Christopher Alleyn, and I wrote to all the constables of this division to notify the taxation of the money for the gaol and the house of correction.

[44] A writ requiring that a specified person be bound to keep the peace.

20 August   The Lord Cobham and I took order for the whipping of Marie Rice and of [blank] Halle, both of Cobham, for a bastard woman child there born of her and begotten by him, and that either of them should pay 8 *d.* by the week towards the finding thereof and the discharge of that parish.

The same day we sent to the house of correction at Maidstone Marie Grafton, for refusing to serve according to her covenant, etc.

A little before, the said Lord and I took order that they of the parish of Meopham should not expel James Butler, who had been conversant there by the space of four years before and did live of honest labor.

24 September   At the quarter sessions at Maidstone I certified the recognizance for the alehouse aforesaid.

4 December   I bound Margaret Mantell, late of Shorne, widow, to the peace against Jane Cowper of the same, widow, in 10 *li.*, and Thomas Allen, her son, of Cliffe, in 5 *li.*, till Easter next following, etc., without appearance, etc.

24 December   Mr. Dr. William Lewin and I took order that Margaret Dutton should be first whipped at Gravesend and then sent to the house of correction for a bastard woman child there born and begotten on her by Robert Cole, as it is thought, whom also we committed till he give sureties to appear at the Easter sessions, for to stand to the order of the bench there, because he refused to perform the order set down against him by my Lord Cobham and Mr. Somer.

The same day also he and I took like order for the whipping of Abigail Sherwood for a bastard man child born by her at Chatham and for her like sending to the house of correction. But as touching the reputed father, we left the decision thereof to the ecclesiastical trial, for that she confessed herself to have been carnally known of many men. The child also was dead so that nothing was to be done in the behalf of the parish.

The same time also he and I bound Thomas Pigeon of Chalk, tippler, with Robert Pigeon and Adrian Walker of Chalk, his two sureties, to appear at the next gaol delivery to answer to two several robberies done the night before at Chalk in the highway.

27 December　Mr. Dr. Lewin and I bound Robert Cole of Gravesend, in 20 *li.*, and Thomas Wright and John Hastelyn of the same, either in 10 *li.*, that Cole should appear at the next quarter sessions at Maidstone and there abide the order that should be taken concerning a bastard which he was charged to have begotten, etc.

1584

6 January　John Lorimer of Gillingham lost two sheep, which Henry Lone of Cooling and John Garret of Higham, laborers, drave away and sold. I bailed Garret by John Goodale and Thomas Goodale of Higham, and Lone by Edward Woodier and Lionel Phips of Cooling, every of them in 5 *li.*, for the appearance of Lone and Garret at the next general gaol delivery.

7 January　I bound Peter Hatcher of Wrotham, yeoman, in 20 *li.*, to appear at the next general gaol delivery in this shire to answer to the death of Francis Wastness, wherewith the Lord Abergavenny charged him.

10 January　Mr. Byng and I took the examination of John Bristow for a burglary laid to his charge by the Lord Abergavenny, and took also the informations against him and made a warrant to commit him.

24 January Mr. Somer and I licensed Thomas Jones to sell ale at the sign of the Gauntlet and Estridge Feather in Upnor Street in the parish of Frindsbury, binding him, in 10 *li.*, and Robert Wardlow and John Lambert, yeomen (warders in Upnor Castle), in 5 *li.* either, with the common condition.

20 February I certified at the gaol delivery at Rochester, 20 February, the examination for Bristow. Peter Hatcher was released by my Lord Abergavenny. Lone and Garret I discharged before, having the opinion of Sir Thomas Gawdy, Justice of Assizes, that their fact was not felony. And Pigeon I also bound over to the next gaol delivery because no man followed the cause against him. At this time I was put in the commission of oyer and terminer.[45]

3 March My Lord Cobham and I by his motion allowed Thomas Hayte of Cobham to sell ale at the sign of the George, near the church stile. He was bound, in 10 *li.*, and Edward Comfort of Chislehurst, yeoman, and John Hayte of Paul's Cray, miller, either in 5 *li.*, with the common condition. This I certified the third day after the next quarter sessions.

14 [March?] I discharged the said Abigail out of the house of correction, taking the promise of William Poldishe of Cranbrook, painter, and of Michael Colgate of Cranbrook, fletcher, in the presence of Elizabeth Sherwood, her mother-in-law, that she should presently be taken into honest service.

20 March Mr. Dr. Lewin and I took order that Alice Trammel of Cliffe should be scourged there for a bastard, whereof [blank] was the reputed father.

24 March I bound William Ward of Higham, husbandman, in 10 *li.*, and John London and John Fuller of the same, his sureties,

[45] Cf. Holdsworth, *op. cit.*, I, 274, 277.

in 5 *li.* each, to keep the peace towards John King of the same, laborer, and to appear, etc. It is released 18 April.

25 March   I bound John King of Higham, laborer, in 10 *li.*, and Benjamin English of Strood, gentleman, and William Peare of the same, yeoman, each in 5 *li.*, to keep the peace towards the said William Ward, etc., and to appear at the next quarter sessions, etc. It is released 18 April 1584.

27 March   I sent to the gaol Derek Stephens for a burglary, and bound, etc., to give evidence.
   The same day I sent to the gaol Joan Reignolds for stealing a frieze gown, and bound, etc., to give in evidence.

7 April   Mr. Thomas Fane and I bailed Jonas Carr, imprisoned for suspicion of felony, binding him, in 20 *li.*, George Parker of Frittenden, clothier, in 20 *li.*, and George Carr of the same, tailor, in 10 *li.*, to appear, etc., after the usual condition.

12 April   I bound Jane Cowper of Shorne, widow, to the peace, in 10 *li.*, with William Hinton of Snodland, wheeler, in 5 *li.*, and Abraham Cokar of the same, tailor, in 5 *li.*, as her sureties, etc., without appearance, but for the peace, till Michaelmas next.

16 April   Mr. Mayor of Maidstone, Mr. Fludd, and I took the examinations of Ed Pine of Maidstone, brazier, touching the stealing of lead from the churches of Barming, Loose, East Peckham, and Bearsted; the Mayor hath them.

28 April   At the quarter sessions at Maidstone I certified the said recognizances of Margaret Mantell, Thomas Jones, William Ward, John King, Jane Cowper, and Robert Cole.

29 April   Sir Christopher Alleyn and I bound John Hunt of West Peckham, yeoman, in 20 *li.*, that Richard Cowper, of whom see before, 1582, 11 December, should pay weekly 6 *d.* according to the order thereof and that he should also pay all the arrearages thereof before the end of twenty days next.

5 May   I sent to the gaol John West for stealing two shirts, three table napkins, two head kerchiefs that day from Richard Hayes of Cobham, whom I bound, in 5 *li.*, that he and Elizabeth, his daughter, should give evidence, etc. With this West I sent Margaret, his wife, and John Wilson as rogues and, perhaps, *criminis participes.*

13 June   Mr. Somer and I took at Cobham Hall the examination of John Poulter and the information against him for a cow and calf stolen from John Miller of Frindsbury. We bailed him by Henry Parker and Henry Wellet and bound John Miller to give evidence, etc.

21 June   I bound John Moss of Snodland, yeoman, to the peace against William Daniel, in 20 *li.*, and John Parmenter, yeoman, and Abraham Cokar, tailor, all of Snodland, either in 10 *li.*, and to appear at the next quarter sessions of the peace at Maidstone. This was certified.

30 June   I sent to the gaol Robert Cook for suspicion of stealing five lambs, and bound Thomas Williams of Chalk to give evidence, etc.

2 July   I bound to the good behavior William Parker, John Barnard, and Leonard Brooker of Gillingham, and afterward discharged them for cony hunting, etc.

13 July   At the gaol delivery holden at Rochester I certified all the informations, examinations, and recognizances aforesaid.

An Ephemeris

26 July I delivered out of the house of correction at Maidstone Margaret Dutton aforesaid unto Robert Startup of Maidstone, who undertook to keep her in service for one whole year, etc.

30 July The Lord Cobham and I bailed Thomas Wilson, 10 *li.*, taken for stealing two sheep, by John Master, 5 *li.*, and Nicholas Child of Meopham, 5 *li.*, until the next gaol delivery, etc.

20 August I sent to the gaol Stephen Upton for stealing divers things out of a house in Cobham.

27 August Mr. Thomas Randolph and I bailed Thomas Ball of Gravesend, taken for stealing money out of another's purse, by William Williams and Richard Biggs until the next gaol delivery, etc.

At the quarter sessions at Maidstone, 22 September, I certified the said recognizance of Moss, the other for good behavior I released.

25 September The Lord Cobham and I bound George Dan, 20 *li.*, Richard Dan, 20 *li.*, and Reuben Colman, 20 *li.*, to appear at the next quarter sessions at Maidstone to answer to their misdemeanor of hunting in Cooling Park.

Ultimo October I bound to the peace Gregory Giles of Cobham, tailor, in 10 *li.*, and William Horden and Walter Henaker of the same, his sureties, yeomen, each in 5 *li.*, against Robert Spryver of Cobham, yeoman, till the next quarter sessions at Maidstone, etc.

7 December I bailed Richard Startup by his master, Thomas Waller, in 5 *li.*, and Richard Acton, in 5 *li.*, both of St. Margaret's, charged with the cutting of a purse.

21 December   I sent to the house of correction Jane Cowper of Shorne at the complaint of the better sort of the parish.

24 December   I bound to the peace at the suit of William Crookshank of Strood, Nicholas Bartholomew, fletcher, 20 *li.*, with William Williams and William Peare, both in 10 *li.*, his sureties, all of Strood, till Easter sessions, etc.

Upon the departure of one of the constables of Shamele I wrote to Reignold Hawkes of Shorne to take the office upon him.

Ultimo December   I bound Robert Crips of Meopham, husbandman, in 20 *li.*, to appear at the quarter sessions after Easter and to answer to the accusation of getting Margery Tailford, late his servant, with child.

1585

2 January   I sent to the gaol as rogues Gabriel Lilly of Yorkshire and John Nicolson of Lincolnshire, brought by John Hawkes, constable.

14 January   I sent to the gaol John Rode, John Sayer, and Edward Williams, charged with robbing of a shop in London. And the 15 of January Mr. Fludd and I bailed John Glassborough of Ryarsh by Thomas Godden and Richard Boorman of the same, yeomen; and John Bartrop of Minster-in-Sheppey by Robert Nynne of Ryarsh, gentleman, and William Wood of Birling, yeoman, the principals in 60 *li.* the piece and the sureties in 40 *li.* the piece, suspected of the same felony.

23 February   I sent to the gaol Jacob Persons and Anne Smith for pilferies done in the house of Pigeon of Cliffe, etc.

25 February   At the assizes holden at Rochester I certified all the causes and recognizances abovesaid that belonged thereto.

7 March   I bound to the peace Thomas Pigeon of Chalk, tippler, 20 *li.*, with Anthony Friend of the same, laborer, 10 *li.*, and Richard Turner of the same, laborer, 10 *li.*, against John Stockwell of Chalk, laborer, and to appear, if I shall call him thereto, at the quarter sessions after Michaelmas 1584 [1585].

8 March   The Lord Abergavenny and I bailed Francis Wastness, 40 *li.*, charged with the suspicion of taking 4 *li.* 10 *s.* from my Lord's baker, Richard Hartrop of Aylesford, yeoman, 20 *li.*, and [blank] Neal of Ditton, yeoman, 20 *li.*, being his sureties, to appear at the gaol delivery, etc.

10 March   I bound Valentine Baker of Aylesford, tailor, in 40 *li.*, George Hickmott of the same, millwright, in 20 *li.*, and Edward Plott of the same, husbandman, in 20 *li.*, that the said Baker shall appear, upon three days' warning given at his house, at any time within one year and a day after Sunday last past to answer concerning the hurt of Nicholas Manser of Aylesford, laborer, done the said Sunday.

14 March   I bound John Vaughan of Halling, tailor, in 20 *li.*, to keep the peace against Edward Chittenden of Snodland, tailor, till the Michaelmas sessions of the peace, 1585. It was released by Chittenden.

19 March   The Lord Cobham and I admitted John London of Higham to keep a victualing house in the High Street there, binding him, in 10 *li.*, and John Goody and Andrew Smith, both of Higham, in 5 *li.* the piece, as his sureties, with the common condition.

The same day Mr. Becher and I took order for the whipping, etc., of Margery Tailford of Meopham for a bastard. And at the Easter sessions the said Robert Crips was charged by 6 *d.* the week towards the finding of that child.

I bound Humphrey Austin of Milton near Gravesend, in 20 *li.*, and Edward Harvey of the same, yeoman, and Thomas Isaac of the same, shoemaker, each in 10 *li.*, to keep the peace against Gilbert Hodgekinson of the same, tailor, with appearances, etc., at the Easter sessions. This was released by Hodgekinson.

22 March I bound to the peace William Cartwright, alias Naylor, of Frindsbury, laborer, in 10 *li.*, and William Pate and Robert Randall of the same, husbandmen, his sureties, each in 5 *li.*, to keep the peace against Susan Skinner, the wife of Stephen Skinner of the same, tailor, and to appear at Michaelmas sessions of the peace.

3 April I bound to the peace (at the suit of Alice, the wife of John Munn of Strood, tippler) Richard Brown, of Strood, tippler, 10 *li.*, and him for Mildred, his wife, with William Wastness of Rochester, gentleman, and John Capon of Rochester, surgeon, for either in 5 *li.* the piece, and to appear, etc.

13 April Thomas Johnson of Northfleet, laborer, 40 *li.*, William Reynes of Mereworth, gentleman, 20 *li.*, Robert Moncastle of the same, yeoman, 20 *li.*, were bound that the said Thomas shall appear at any time within one year next after the Annunciation 1585, upon seven days' warning given at the now house of the said William Reynes.

14 April I bound Thomas Kemp of Aylesford, carpenter, in 40 *li.*, and Richard Rayfield and William Rayfield, both of Burham, yeomen, each in 20 *li.*, to appear and answer, as Valentine Baker before, and for the same cause.

20 April At the quarter sessions at Maidstone I certified all the recognizances aforesaid, except Austin's, Giles's, and Bartholomew's, which were discharged. And Cartwright's I reserve till Michaelmas sessions, as also Pigeon's and Vaughan's.

24 April I sent to the gaol John Atkinson, charged with the felony of taking 34 *li.* 12 *s.* 9 *d.* in money, and bound John Phillips of Canterbury, carrier, in 100 marks, and Christopher Tompson of Gravesend, in 20 *li.*, to give evidence at the next gaol delivery.

26 April I delivered out of the house of correction Margery Tailford, committed thither by Mr. Becher and me.

28 April I sent to the gaol George Preble of Allhallows, laborer, charged with words touching the change of the estate of the realm.

I bound to the peace Anthony Robinson of Frindsbury, miller, 20 *li.*, and Humphrey Reignolds of Rochester, butcher, 10 *li.*, and Thomas Mitchell, of the same, hackney man, 10 *li.*, his sureties, against John Collier of Frindsbury, miller, and to appear at the Michaelmas quarter sessions. The said John Collier released the said surety, 29 May 1585.

31 May David Ray of East Malling, cooper, informed that Francis Hancock of New Hythe there failed to serve upon the amendment of the highways there upon Tuesday or Wednesday last, and evil entreated the said Ray, being a surveyor. Whereupon I bound the said Ray, in 10 *li.*, to appear at the next quarter sessions and to give this matter in evidence.

May The Lord Abergavenny and I committed to the gaol William Mountford for want of sureties for his good behavior.

5 July At the gaol delivery holden at Maidstone, 5 July 1585, I certified the examinations, etc., concerning Atkinson and Preble, and Francis Wastness was discharged by the Lord Abergavenny.

6 July And there I bound Hugh Wilson of Higham, purveyor, in 40 *li.*, to appear at the next quarter sessions at Maidstone, and [blank] in [blank] to give evidence against him. Send to Mr. Becher for the examinations, etc.

I bound [blank] Tresse, borsholder of Stansted, to appear at the next quarter sessions at Maidstone for suffering Thomas Tottel to go, etc. Released by my Lord Abergavenny.

3 August The Lord Cobham and I bound William Chambers and John Owen, both of Strood, each in 20 *li.*, and John Nicolson and Thomas Williams, their several sureties, each for each in 10 *li.*, for the appearance of Chambers and Owen at the next quarter sessions and in the meantime to be of good behavior. It was for hunting my Lord's conies, whose man, Bacon, can give the evidence, etc. But he released it, etc.

5 August Mr. Leveson and I bound to the peace Thomas Pettit of Shorne, smith, 20 *li.*, with John Hutchin and Service Frank, both of Shorne, yeomen, each in 10 *li.*, at the suit of William Wyatt of Higham, laborer, and to appear at the quarter sessions. This was released at Shorne, 18 September.

13 August I examined Thomas Lewes of London, linen draper, upon the statute of hue and cry (27 Elizabeth, ca. 13) concerning a robbery done upon him, as he said, 3 January last, who answered negatively, etc.

15 August I took the confession of Richard Barton concerning the burglary done by him and Thomas Tottel at Birling in the Lord Abergavenny's house 28 March before, and committed him to Maidstone gaol.

12 September I sent to the gaol Thomas Weaver of Cobham, charged with the suspicion of robbing a house there, and bound Nicholas Poore of Cobham to give evidence.

26 September   Edward Millet of Strood, tailor, informed me of a composition made between Thomas Harris of Cobham and him and one John Champ for 4 *li.* to be paid concerning certain cloth stolen out of the shop of the said Harris at Cobham, of the privity whereof the said Champ and Millet were accused by one that was executed.

28 September   At the quarter sessions holden at Maidstone I certified the recognizances aforesaid that were not released before.

3 October   Mr. Leveson and I sent to the house of correction John Mansell of Strood, glover, for getting a bastard upon [blank], widow, of the same.

4 December   I bound to the peace John King of Higham, laborer, 20 *li.*, with William Rolfe, 10 *li.*, and John Hote, 10 *li.*, at the suit of Thomas Newman, all of Higham aforesaid, till the Easter sessions next, and to appear, etc. He released it.

5 December   Mr. Leveson and I sent to the gaol at Maidstone James Tomsett for a burglary done that night before at Meopham, and bound Timothy Scudder, in 20 *li.*, to give evidence, etc.

8 December   I bound to the peace William Waite of Cobham, shoemaker, in 10 *li.*, with Gilbert Young of Cobham, yeoman, in 5 *li.*, and John Horden of Cobham, weaver, in 5 *li.*, to keep the peace against Vincent Waite of Luddesdown, yeoman, and to appear at the next Easter sessions, etc. He released it.

1586

16 February   I bound George Tucker the younger of Milton, 100 *li.*, and his two sureties, William Clark of the same, 100 marks, and William Brown of Gravesend, 100 marks, that the said George shall be forthcoming at any time within a year and day after to answer to the wounding of Humphrey Austin of Milton aforesaid.

21 February At the assizes then holden at Rochester I certified all the recognizances and examinations thereto belonging.

22 February Mr. Leveson and I committed to the gaol Sara Gold of St. Margaret's for destroying her child whereof she was delivered that day. Ask of Mr. Coates, the coroner, for the information of the midwife, of Mrs. Swalman, and Anthony Simpkins.

28 February Mr. Leveson, Mr. Becher, and I sent to the gaol William Cokar of Halling for keeping an alehouse and maintaining play at the dice of his own authority. Remember his recognizance and the certificate of his offense to the next sessions.

1 March I sent to the house of correction Edward Long, late of Loose, for offering fear to such as dwelt alone, etc.

14 March Mr. Leveson and I bound George Dan of Allhallows, 20 *li.*, and Thomas Davies of the same, yeoman, 20 *li.*, with their sureties, John Stretton, sailor, and John Atwood of the same, yeoman, severally in 10 *li.* for either of the other twain, for the good behavior and appearance, etc. It was discharged.

24 March I sent to the gaol Thomas Hall of Halling, for stealing certain money and other things, and I bound Nicholas Nicholas of Halling, 10 *li.*, to give evidence, etc.

An Ephemeris

6 April   Mr. Leveson and I sent to the house of correction Margery White of Rochester, for one month, for a bastard and for refusing to work.

The same day he and I bound to the peace Robert Crips of Meopham, yeoman, 20 *li.*, with his sureties, Thomas Kennet and John Wright of the same, yeomen, 10 *li.*, to keep the peace against Robert Smith of the same, etc. He released it.

8 April   Mr. Becher and I sent to the gaol John Dan of St. Mary's, charged with the death of Margaret Harding, his wench. John Jenkin and [blank] were bound to give evidence. But Mr. Becher hath the examinations and bond, and the coroner will deal with the cause.

I bound the said Robert Crips to appear as before, to answer to his contempt for not paying the weekly 6 *d.* towards the finding of the bastard aforesaid.

12 April   At the quarter sessions I certified the recognizance of Cokar, etc.

13 April   Mr. Leveson and I bound to the good behavior and appearance Thomas Gatford, 10 *li.*, with his sureties, John London, 5 *li.*, and George Frank, 5 *li.*, all of Higham, yeomen.[46]

19 April   I bound Edward Gilvin of Wouldham, fisherman, 10 *li.*, to the peace, and Walter Browman of Wouldham, yeoman, his surety, 5 *li.*, and them both for Elizabeth his wife, at the suit of Frances Tompson of the same, spinster, and for their appearance, etc.[47]

---

[46] This entry is crossed out in the manuscript, which contains a briefer account of the same matter before a similarly abbreviated duplicate entry for April 19. Both are entered out of the proper chronological order. Since they are merely repetitions, both duplicate entries are omitted.

[47] Crossed out in the manuscript, just as the preceding one.

27 June To the gaol delivery at Rochester I certified the recognizance of Nicholas Nicholas, etc.

17 July I took the information of Matthew Bridges of Denton, gentleman, against Joan Myles of London, for stealing apparel from Paul Baker of the Old Bailey of London, gentleman, and bound the said Matthew to give evidence at Newgate; and I sent the prisoner and the whole cause to Mr. Recorder of London by Russel, the borsholder of Gravesend.

21 July Mr. Leveson and I sent to the gaol Robert Cook for stealing a sow and seven pigs, and bound William Hoff of Halstow, 10 *li.*, and Richard Brown of Strood, 5 *li.*, to give evidence.

25 July Mr. Leveson and I, by appointment of the Lord Cobham, licensed Robert Kirby of Shorne to keep victualing, binding him in 10 *li.*, and Reignold Hawkes and John Mitchell, his sureties, both of Shorne, each in 5 *li.*, for the keeping of good rule and order, etc.

18 August Mr. Leveson and I bound Roger Somerland of Milton, innholder, 10 *li.*, to the peace against William Bennet of the same, with Thomas Tuttesham, gentleman, 5 *li.*, and Reignold Hawkes of Shorne, yeoman, 5 *li.*, his sureties, etc., to appear at the next quarter sessions at Maidstone.

29 August I sent to the gaol Thomas Cockes, late of Strood, tinker, for robbing the house of Alice Fuller, widow, and bound her, in 5 *li.*, to give evidence, etc.

20 September I bound to the peace Henry Smith of Southfleet, husbandman, 20 *li.*, with Ralph Metcalf of the same, gentleman, 10 *li.*, to keep the peace against Richard Dew of the same, tailor, and to appear, etc.

23 November I bound Laurence Grinnell of Milton near Gravesend, hosteler, 10 *li.*, and his master, Christopher Barnard of the same, innholder, in 5 *li.*, as his surety, that Laurence shall appear at the next quarter sessions of the peace at Maidstone or before me at any time before upon warning, and to be of good behavior. It was for begetting a bastard, etc., which died.

9 December Mr. Leveson, Mr. Becher, and I licensed John London of Higham to keep an alehouse there, binding him, in 10 *li.*, and John Woodgreen and Thomas Cooper, his sureties, either in 5 *li.*, with the common condition.

The same day Mr. Becher and I joined in putting down the alehouse of Thomas Hayte of Cobham.

15 December Mr. Sedley and I bailed John Poulter of Northfleet, 20 *li.*, charged with stealing a bushel of wheat, by his sureties, Richard Parker and William Swan of the same, gentlemen, each in 10 *li.*, and the examinations of George Rettewell and John Prior Mr. Sedley hath.

23 December Mr. Becher and I bound Ralph Batty of Rainham, miller, in 30 *li.*, to pay 10 *d.* weekly or to discharge them of Gillingham for a bastard named Ralph Batty begotten by him there on the body of Joan Harding of Gillingham, and her we ordered to be whipped at Gillingham. Mr. Becher hath this obligation.

1587

10 January I bound to the good behavior Elizabeth Watson of Halling, widow, 20 *li.*, with William Symons, 10 *li.*, and Henry Bray, of the same, yeoman, 10 *li.*, to appear at the next quarter sessions at Maidstone and to be in the meanwhile of good behavior. I released it.

19 January   Mr. Thomas Fane, Mr. William Sedley, Mr. Edward Becher, and I bailed out of the gaol William Wood, a cook, 40 *li.*, sent thither by the Lord Abergavenny *ad respondend super hiis,* etc., by James Dowle of East Malling, fuller, 20 *li.*, and Thomas Godden of Paddlesworth, yeoman, 20 *li.*, till the next general gaol delivery.

24 January   Mr. Becher and I bailed Simon Halle of Milton near Gravesend, baker, 100 *li.*, charged with the manslaughter of Robert Lee of the same, baker, by Thomas Mayhoe of the same, gentleman, 50 *li.*, and Robert Martin of the same, baker, 50 *li.*, to appear at the next general gaol delivery and to be of good behavior in the mean season.

23 February   Mr. Leveson and I licensed and bound Thomas Pigeon of Chalk, 10 *li.*, for victualing, by his sureties, George Wright, gentleman, of Cobham, 5 *li.*, and Peter Millar of Gravesend, brewer, 5 *li.*

25 February   Mr. Leveson, Mr. Becher, and I sat upon a riot at Meopham, where Thomas Wombwell, gentleman, and six others were indicted, whose fines were assessed to 3 *li.* in all, and bound him for payment thereof. We then also bound him and William Reynes to the peace mutually.

3 April   Henry Jackson of Gillingham, fisherman, 20 *li.*, for himself and Joan, his wife, with William Symons of Halling, 10 *li.*, and John Wood of the same, 10 *li.*, were bound to keep the peace against Richard Wissenden of Gillingham, butcher, and to appear, etc.

Alehouses   Mr. Leveson, Mr. Becher, and I joined in setting up these alehouses following: viz., John Brown, James Beer, Robert Harrison, of Gravesend; Robert Squire, Roger Somerland, Robert Martin, of Milton; Thomas Pilchard of Gillingham; [blank] Russe of Cobham.

25 April At the quarter sessions at Maidstone we certified all the said recognizances for peace, alehouses, etc., and delivered in the record of the said riot, etc.

23 June We of this division sent out towards the Low Countries thirteen men for our part of fifty men allotted to this lathe of Aylesford; given to every one 2 *s.* press money and to the captain 10 *d.* for each one towards coat and furniture; the whole shire made out three hundred.

26 June I sent to the gaol John Crondal of Gravesend, miller, charged with the stealing of malt, and Elizabeth, the wife of Robert Cole, as accessory thereto, and bound Peter Millar of Gravesend, brewer, in 10 *li.*, and Joan Monney of the same, in 10 *li.*, to give evidence, etc.

1 July Mr. Leveson and I bailed the said Elizabeth Cole by her said husband, 20 *li.*, and William Symons of Halling, 20 *li.*, to appear at the next gaol delivery.

2 July Mr. Leveson and I bailed Collinson [blank] of Wateringbury, borsholder, by [blank] Codd and [blank] Barham.

10 July To the gaol delivery at Maidstone I certified the bails and recognizances, etc., aforesaid.

12 July The last day of the assizes I sent to the gaol John Smith for stealing a gelding, and bound John Foot of Battle in Sussex, 40 *li.*, to give evidence, etc., and William Orrel, servant to Mr. Edward Gage of Sussex.

18 July I sent to the gaol Robert Giles and James Hopkins for burglary and stealing ten yards of raw cloth, and I bound Edward Leeds, 10 *li.*, and [blank] Everinden, 10 *li.*, to give evidence, etc.

28 July I bound Stephen Grove of Addington, carpenter, and George Durrock of Offham, carpenter, and Edward Gray of Town Malling, laborer, each two for the other, in 10 *li.* apiece, to appear upon two days' warning, for hunting of conies in Birling Park.

2 August I bound Nevil Reeve of Aylesford, gentleman, 200 *li.*, with Henry Warcop of the same, gentleman, 100 *li.*, and Richard Reeve of Maidstone, innholder, 100 *li.*, that Nevil shall appear at the next general gaol delivery, etc., and in the meantime be of good port and behavior. It was for the hurting of Thomas Reynes of Burham, yeoman, with a stone, to the peril of death, as it is said, etc. Released by Reynes.

4 August Robert Reeve, late of London, gentleman, was by me bound, in 100 *li.*, to appear at the next quarter sessions at Maidstone for the cause last abovesaid, by desire of Thomas Reynes.

31 August Josias Milles, sawyer, charged with the picking of a purse, was suffered to escape by William Waite of Cobham, borsholder, etc. Look the examination. He was sent to the gaol, being taken again 19 September 1587.

14 September Mungra Russel, a Scot, charged to beget a woman child upon Rebecca Gore of East Malling, was by me sent to the gaol for not finding sureties for his good behavior and appearance, etc. Send for old Gore, her father, etc. He is escaped. Send for James Dowle, the borsholder.

2 October I sent to the gaol John Jennings, loader, for stealing wheat from his master, Thomas Duke, Esquire, and I bound John Burchall in 10 *li.*, to give evidence.

An Ephemeris

3 December   I sent to the house of correction Thomas Bachelor and David Smith of this shire, wandering minstrels, etc., for six days.

10 December   William Reignolds, butcher, 10 *li.*, John Parmenter, yeoman, 5 *li.*, and Thomas Barnard, tailor, 5 *li.*, all of Snodland, bound that William Reignolds shall be of good behavior till Shrove Sunday next.

19 December   I sent to the gaol Thomas Smith of Malling, tailor, charged with counterfeiting money and stealing of money from Nicholas Gould there, and bound him, William Ayhurst, William Barret, Marie Alphrey, and others to give evidence.

1588

2 January   I bound to the good behavior Thomas Vaughan of Snodland, loader, 20 *li.*, with his sureties, William Elfye the elder, of Birling, 10 *li.*, and Thomas Tunbridge of the same, 10 *li.*, and to appear at the next Easter sessions, for a bastard.

4 January   I sent to the gaol Richard Hart for stealing money, spoons, etc. I have bound John Cotwell, in 20 *li.*, to give evidence.

8 January   John Poore of Luddesdown was licensed to sell ale and beer, being bound in 10 *li.*, and Richard Waite and Richard Cosin of the same, each in five pounds, with the common condition.

11 January   I bound to appear at the next Easter sessions at Maidstone John Crowhurst of Aylesford, laborer, 20 *li.*, and Thomas Reynes of Burham, yeoman, 10 *li.*, touching the begetting with child of Agnes Cumber of East Malling.

17 April   I bound them over till the next Michaelmas sessions. Order is taken.

22 February   To the gaol delivery at Sevenoaks I certified the informations, examinations, and recognizances thereto belonging.

8 March   Mr. Becher and I took order at Strood church for the arrearages of the composition wheat in this division.[48]

9 March   I bound to the good behavior and to appear at the Easter sessions John May of Malling, tailor, 20 *li.*, with his sureties, John Mayo of the same, tailor, 10 *li.*, and John Kipping of the same, smith, 10 *li.*

16 March   I sent to the gaol Marie, the wife of John Alphrey of West Malling, gentleman, for misprision of the treason and procuring the burglary of Thomas Smith aforesaid.

To the quarter sessions at Maidstone I certified the said recognizances thereto belonging, 16 April.

26 April   I bound to the peace and the next quarter sessions Richard Cook of Milton, victualer, 20 *li.*, with his sureties, Thomas Layston, 10 *li.*, and Roger Somerland, 10 *li.*, towards [blank] Clark there.

6 June, 7 June   Mr. Leveson and I took order for John Vaughan, a bastard child, begotten at Birling by Thomas Vaughan of Snodland, miller, on Marion Gorby, widow, of Birling also, which

---

[48] Probably composition for royal rights of purveyance. Kent was among the last counties to compound. The county compounded for wheat before 1591 but not for other provisions before 1602. It would appear from this entry that Kent had compounded for wheat as early as 1588. See Allegra Woodworth, *Purveyance in the Royal Household* (Transactions of the American Philosophical Society, new ser., XXXV, Pt. 1 [1945]), pp. 40–41, 81.

Thomas, with John Coveney and William Elfye, all of Birling, were bound, in 30 *li.*, to save the parish harmless. Mr. Leveson hath the bond.

He and I took order also for Agnes Cumber, a bastard begotten on Agnes Cumber of East Malling by John Crowhurst of Aylesford, with the like bond of them and of Thomas Reynes of Burham, yeoman, for discharge of East Malling. And we ordered all the said four offenders to be whipped in the open market of West Malling, 8 June 1588.

8 June　I bound Francis Leafe of Milton, smith, to appear at the next gaol delivery, touching certain raw cloths taken from Alfy of Godmersham.

14 June　I sent to the gaol John Pagdene for suspicion of felony, and bound George Boorman to give evidence.

The same day I sent to the gaol John Lewis, late of Cliffe, tailor, for suspicion of burglary of the house of William Barry of Stoke, and bound him, in 10 *li.*, to give evidence.

22 June　I bound George Wright of Cobham, gentleman, in 100 *li.*, to keep the peace against John Beer of Gravesend, jurat,[49] and to appear at the next quarter sessions at Maidstone. This, was released.

27 June　I bound to the peace William Simpkins of the College of Rochester, 20 *li.*, with Henry Huggins of Wouldham, 10 *li.*, and Thomas Symons of Halling, 10 *li.*, to keep the peace against Roper Blundell of the said College and to appear, etc., and I gave him a *supersedeas.*[50] It is released.

---

[49] In Kent members of the town council were called jurats. This whole entry is crossed out in the manuscript.

[50] A writ staying any other officer from taking action against Simpkins for the same cause. Cf. *Eirenarcha*, p. 95.

30 June   I bound John Barton, 20 *li.*, John London, 10 *li.*, and William White, 10 *li.*, all of Higham, his sureties, for the peace and appearance.

1 July   I certified to the gaol delivery at Rochester all the examinations, informations, and recognizances thereto belonging.

2 July   I bound to the peace and to appear Robert Hodshall of Stansted, 40 *li.*, with his sureties, George Wright of Cobham, 20 *li.*, and Robert Hodshall of Kemsing, for himself and Conyes, his wife.

23 July   I bound to the good behavior and appearance, etc., John Christelet of Shorne, 20 *li.*, with Hugh Taylor of Cuxton, yeoman, 20 *li.*, and Ralph Hogsted of Shorne, collar maker, 20 *li.*

1 September   Mr. Leveson and I bound John Thystlow of Strood, thatcher, 20 *li.*, and Giles Collin [perhaps Collier] of Frindsbury, 10 *li.*, and Brian Shoebury of Cuxton, yeoman, 10 *li.*, his sureties, that John shall appear upon a day's warning, etc.

23 [*September?*]   I bound George Wright abovesaid till Easter sessions for the peace towards John Beer in 100 *li.*

24 September   I certified to the quarter sessions at Maidstone all the said recognizances for the peace except that of George Wright.

From henceforth I used another ephemeris.

Charges to Juries

and Commissions

Introduction

AMONG the Lambarde manuscripts that the Folger Library acquired at the sale of 1924 are twenty-nine speeches written in Lambarde's autograph for delivery in Kent between 1582 and 1601. Nineteen of these are charges to juries at the Court of Quarter Sessions held at Maidstone. Of the remaining ten, six are charges to special juries summoned at Maidstone (1581/82) and Town Malling (1592) to deal with riots, at Frindsbury (1586/87) and Strood (1594) to deal with a dearth of corn, and at Maidstone (1582 and 1583) to deal with idle rogues. There are besides two speeches addressed to special commissions set up evidently by order from the Crown. One of these (1595; place unknown) had to do with the periodic search for what were known as "concealed lands," that is to say, lands held from the Crown *in capite* and liable to various feudal incidents, notably wardship, arising out of their tenure.[1] The other (Maidstone,

[1] Cf. H. E. Bell, *An Introduction to the History and Records of the Court of Wards and Liveries* (Cambridge, 1953), p. 3; see below p. 176. Lambarde's connection with these matters does not appear. There is no evidence that he was either an escheator or feodary, the two royal offices chiefly involved. An inquisition post mortem was ordinarily held by the escheator, assisted by a jury impaneled by the sheriff. But in some cases it was made by a royally appointed commission (Bell, *op. cit.*, pp. 72–73).

55

1593/94) had to do with the investigation of corruption in the management of endowed almshouses. Finally, there are two speeches to local inquisitions post mortem (places unknown, 1596, 1600).

Evidently Lambarde was a kind of *bonne à toute faire* for the Crown in Kent. He was not only a J.P. and of the quorum, he was at various times a commissioner of sewers for the Medway, an assistant in the taking of musters, a commissioner for investigating concealed lands, and a commissioner for the investigation of corruption in the management of corporate trusts. And he managed to find time when engaged in all these matters to write the best contemporary account of the English courts of justice (*Archion*, 1635), the history of his county (*A Perambulation of Kent*, 1576), the standard handbook for the justice of the peace (*Eirenarcha*, 1581), and another handbook for town and hundred officers (*The Duties of Constables, Borsholders, etc.*, 1583), and to publish a collection of Anglo-Saxon laws (*Archaionomia*, 1568). In most of his official connections he appears as a spokesman for the Crown. Evidently he was highly regarded in that capacity, though his one recorded speech in the House of Commons nearly led to his undoing.[2]

The most enlightening of these speeches which follow are the ones delivered at quarter sessions as a prologue to the formal charge to the grand jury, a long affair which fills some seventy-five pages in the several editions of *Eirenarcha*. Lambarde himself admits that even in an abbreviated form the charge took two hours to read. He calls these prologues exhortations. They extend over twenty years, from 1582 to Easter 1601. The last of them is endorsed "not used." It may be that Lambarde was not well enough to deliver it. He died in August of that year.

Since a charge was delivered to the grand jury at every meeting of quarter sessions, and since, presumably, Lambarde regularly

[2] See above, p. 9.

prefaced the charge with an exhortation, it is clear that the speeches which survive hardly amount to a quarter of the speeches delivered. He may of course have used the same exhortation more than once; certainly he employed the same phraseology over and over again. But these seem to be all that survive. Unfortunately there appears to have been no inventory of the Lambarde papers that were sold in 1924 and no record kept of the purchasers of the different items offered. Maybe some lucky fellow will come upon others, as I, more or less by chance, came upon those in the Folger Library.[3]

So far as I know, these are the only extant speeches of their kind for Elizabeth's reign. The draft of one, presumably intended for delivery before the quarter sessions in Wiltshire, is preserved among the Thynne Papers at Longleat.[4] It may be that the practice was an uncommon one. Lambarde himself speaks of it in *Eirenarcha* as customary earlier in the old eyre courts and in the assize courts and expresses the wish that it might be introduced at quarter sessions.[5] He may have been responsible for its introduction in Kent.

In Wiltshire quarter sessions, the charge to the grand jury was usually given by the Custos Rotulorum or someone he appointed.[6] The evidence is much too scanty to justify the assumption that the same was true in Kent. We do not even know who was the Custos Rotulorum in Kent when Lambarde delivered his first

[3] The Folger Library acquired later (1951) another Lambarde manuscript, first offered for sale in 1924. It is Lambarde's draft of that part of his *Archion* which deals with Star Chamber. Cf. *Archeion,* ed. Charles L. McIlwain and Paul L. Ward (Cambridge, Mass., 1957), p. 151, n. 12.

[4] Printed in full in *Wiltshire Archaeological and Natural History Magazine,* XIV (1874), 208 ff. It is undated but covers much the same ground as Lambarde's exhortations, though laying much more stress upon religious problems.

[5] *Eirenarcha,* pp. 404–405; see below, p. 103.

[6] The office of Custos Rotulorum and the Lord Lieutenancy were sometimes held by the same person. Cf. Robert Essex in Staffordshire, Burghley in Lincolnshire.

exhortation, but it was probably Thomas Wotton,[7] who was sheriff of Kent in 1558 and again twenty years later, and who was certainly Custos Rotulorum in 1584. Wotton was on the commission of the peace in Kent and one of Lambarde's good friends. Lambarde indeed dedicated his *Perambulation of Kent* to him, "who," he writes, "for the good understanding and interest you have in the shire can, as well as any other, discern of this doing." [8] Probably Wotton held the position and appointed Lambarde to deliver the charges to the grand jury.

The grand jury in Kent, by Lambarde's own account, was made up of two constables of the hundred [9] (sometimes called the high constables to distinguish them from the petty parish constables) together with some others. They were customarily impaneled by the sheriff from the small gentry,[10] but it is evident from one of Lambarde's speeches that the constables were often men of very little property and without the rudiments of education. In April 1599 he observes:

I wish, therefore, first, that none be suffered to occupy the place of constable over an hundred but such only as can both write and read and is withal assessed to the subsidy at 6 or 8 *li.* in lands, or at the double thereof in goods at the least, to the end that by the one he may be able to read and write warrants without discovery of his enjoined service to any other for their help therein, which is the breakneck of many a good business, and by the other he may be sufficient to answer for his fault, seeing that at this day nothing more than beggary emboldeneth to offense.[11]

---

[7] Father of the better-known Sir Edward and Sir Henry Wotton. Wotton died in 1587. Who was Custos Rotulorum between his death and 1596 does not appear.

[8] From the epistle dedicatory, Wotton was certainly related to Lady Burghley.

[9] *Eirenarcha,* p. 398.

[10] Wallace Notestein, *The English People on the Eve of Colonization, 1603–1630* (New York, 1954), p. 236, says that they were appointed by the J.P.'s. Lambarde speaks of them as impaneled by the sheriff and blames him for not furnishing more sufficient jurors.

[11] See below, p. 138.

Introduction to Charges

These exhortations are for the most part critical of the performance of the jurors. Lambarde tells them that they have been refusing to indict their "betters," have favored their friends, and sought vengeance against their enemies. "Spare not," he charges them, "for love, dare not for hatred, stick not for fear." It is, he insists, no part of their business to judge, but solely to present.[12] Twice he points out that at sessions over a ten-year period they had never presented as many cases as there were articles in any of the formal charges.[13]

Sometimes Lambarde appeals to their self-interest in a well-ordered state, sometimes to their patriotism. Sometimes he hints at Star Chamber proceedings against them. On three occasions he threatens to call another jury "to inquire of your willful concealment and, that discovered, to proceed by fine and ransom to the punishment of you." [14]

In commenting upon the shortcomings of the jurors, Lambarde calls attention to the kind of cases with which quarter sessions normally was called upon to deal. He speaks of the disorders of alehouses, which he designates "nurseries of naughtiness," the harborers of vagabonds, the breeding ground of bastards. He speaks of unlawful gaming by day and of untimely walking by night. He speaks of unseemly apparel; he speaks of those who take livery from some great neighbor,[15] pointing out that what the patron saves for his client in the assessment of taxes, in musters, and in other charges, the jurors themselves, like all other members of the community, will have to meet. He speaks

---

[12] See below, pp. 120, 125–126, 139.   [13] See below, pp. 93, 111.
[14] See below, pp. 74, 93, 121; *Eirenarcha*, p. 401; on shortness of sessions, cf. *Eirenarcha*, p. 606.
[15] In this connection an entry in a parliamentary diary of 1624 is pertinent. It is dated April 27, 1624, and runs as follows: "Sir Edward Coke said that he found, whilst he was a judge, that the badge and livery of a justice of the peace or a great man did sway much with jurors when they were either to inquire of any misdemeanor or to give up their verdict in any business and so was a great hindrance of justice." From a transcript in the possession of Wallace Notestein. I owe this reference to Dr. Elizabeth Foster.

of regraters, engrossers, and forestallers, who force up the price of corn. He speaks of those who use false weights and measures. He says nothing of more blatant offenders—felons, murderers, and suchlike. The offenses which he enumerates are not those of the obvious criminals but those countenanced and too often practiced by reputable Englishmen; those contrary to law but not clearly contrary to public morals; those which sometimes, as he put it, "creep in under a veil and cloak of conscience to do well." [16] Lambarde calls them the "roots and first springs of all these evils that infest and trouble the country." [17]

It is rather remarkable that Lambarde's speeches make little or no reference to national problems as distinct from local ones. We hear little of religious issues until the last decade of the reign. It is only in passing that he alludes to conspiracies against the Crown, even in January, 1587,[18] when Mary Stuart has been condemned and is awaiting execution. The coming of the Armada in the summer of 1588 passes unnoticed.

In 1585 Lambarde is expatiating upon the blessings of peace.[19] In the spring of 1586, a few months after Elizabeth has dispatched an army to the Low Countries, he begins to speculate upon the evils of war:

For now such men as have more valor in their bodies than virtue in their minds will think that all the labor lieth on their hands and will therefore grow insolent and boldly adventure upon the breach of laws in hope that (for the necessity that we have of their service) they may not only escape punishment but pass without controlment for it. Now will your sons and servants strive to draw their necks out of the yoke of due obedience. Now will loiterers and idle persons think themselves warranted to walk at their wills. Now will beastly drunkards and blasphemers vaunt that they be valiant and serviceable men. Yea, now will thieves and robbers take upon them as if they were the only soldiers of the world. And therefore, as there is never

[16] See below, p. 127.   [17] See below, p. 70.
[18] See below, pp. 162–163.   [19] See below, p. 78.

more need to use the bridle than when the horse sheereth, so now (above all other times) it is necessary for us to take the bridle of the laws into our own hands.[20]

Much of what he says in subsequent speeches turns upon the disorders of war. He discourses at length upon the problem of the vagrant soldier and explains why it has never arisen before.[21] He points out that in earlier wars the armies were made up of the lords and their retainers, all of whom resumed their peace-time pursuits when the war was over. But now, "when not only our gaols are scoured and our highways swept but also the cannels of our streets be raked for soldiers, what marvel is it if after their return from the wars they do either lead their lives in beggary or end them by hanging."

On another occasion, in 1596, when Englishmen were deeply embroiled both in the Low Countries and in France, he observes:

Since the time that our nation hath conversed with foreign people in the wars abroad, what Frenchman so garish and light in apparel, what Dutchman so daily drunken and given to the pot, what Irish more idle and thievishly disposed, what Scot more cowardly, sudden, and ready to stab, what Spaniard more insolent, fleshly, or blasphemous than be a many of our own English, who have not only learned and transported hither all these vices of those other men, but are grown so perniciously cunning therein that they excel their teachers and teach it to others at home! [22]

Quite evidently Lambarde shared the English despite of the foreigner which had found expression over a century earlier in *The Libel of English Policy.*

During the nineties Lambarde was much concerned about the problem of poverty. In a long discourse on the subject in 1594 he undertakes to explain the reasons for the increase of poverty. He

[20] See below, p. 84. [21] See below, pp. 183–184.
[22] See below, pp. 129–130.

attributes it in large measure to the increase of population due, on the positive side, to the earlier marriages of the young and to the marriage of the clergy and, on the negative side, to the reduction of the death rate because "we have not, God be thanked, been touched with any extreme mortality, either by sword or sickness." The rise of prices and of rents, and the "cancerous sore of daily usury, which is already run and spread over all the body of the commonwealth," he holds to be other factors—vagrant soldiers, of course, another. With the normal xenophobia of the time, he ascribes poverty to the increasing indulgence in expensive foreign commodities.[23] It apparently never occurred to Lambarde that an important factor in unemployment was the disturbance of the foreign market, upon which English prosperity increasingly depended.[24]

Lambarde's most eloquent passages are in praise of English justice:

The times hath been when the nobility and commons of this realm have (with all humility and heart's desire) begged at the hands of their princes the continuation of their country laws and customs; and not prevailing so, they have armed themselves and have sought by force and with the adventure of their honors, goods, and lives to extort it from them. But we (God's name be blessed for it) do live in such a time and under such a prince as we need not to make suit, much less to move war, for our country laws and liberties. We have no cause to strive so much and so long about Magna Charta, the Great Charter of England, as it was called. For our prince hath therein already prevented us, so that not only the parts of that Great Charter but also many other laws and statutes no less fit and profitable for us than they are freely yielded unto us, and that not to be fetched afar off by us but sent home by her even to our own doors;

[23] See below, p. 182.
[24] William R. Scott, *The Constitution and Finance of English, Scottish, and Irish Joint-Stock Companies* (Cambridge, 1910–12), I, 97–98; Lawrence Stone, "Elizabethan Overseas Trade," *Economic History Review*, 2nd ser., II (1949), 43 ff.

not to be administered by foreign judges and spies but by our own friends, familiars, and countrymen.[25]

On another occasion he protests that the failure of the juries to perform their functions has forced the government to provide other methods of enforcing the law—the Star Chamber without the use of any jury, the hearing and determining of cases by the justices of the peace without jury, the flourishing numbers of promoters and informers ("like flies that feed upon the sores of diseased cattle"), the new invention of provost marshal "to rake our rogues together."

Thus you see how by the only default of jurors and inquests the native liberty and ancient preëminence of the English policy is already by little and little exceedingly shred off and diminished, very like also in short time to be utterly lost and taken from us if you lay not better hands and hold upon it. Which thing if it should happen in our days (as God forbid that it ever happen at all) we shall be condemned by all posterity to have been the most ungracious and base-minded age of men that have lived here since the general conquest of our nation and country.

His final words have something of the ring of Sir John Eliot about them:

Stand fast, therefore, stand fast, I say, in this liberty whereunto you are born and be inheritable. Show yourselves to have before your eyes a fear of God, a conscience of your oaths, an obedience to your prince, a love to your country, and an earnest desire to leave safe and sound to your children and offspring this inestimable jewel and precious patrimony of a most liberal, easy, and sure law which your forefathers, not without sweat and blood, have recovered and left to descend upon you.[26]

CONYERS READ

[25] See below, p. 79. [26] See below, p. 108.

CHARGES TO JURIES
AT QUARTER SESSIONS

Charges to Quarter Sessions

ૐ

A Charge for the General Sessions
of the Peace
Uttered 24 April 1582, at Maidstone

Such is the perversity of the common nature of us all that whereas the often repetition of one thing should, by all reason and likelihood, so beat the same into our minds as it should make the deeper impression thereof in our hearts, we contrariwise do by custom of hearing wax negligent of that which is told us, and howsoever weighty the thing be of itself we through daily acquaintance with it do receive and use it but as a verse of course, and do suffer it swiftly to run through our heads. And this fault of ours followeth us, not only in things pertaining to the world, but also in matters concerning God Himself. For, to pass over other things, what prayers, I beseech you (if we will each man examine it in his own), are more coldly or with less care and devotion uttered by us than even those which we do daily and most accustomably conceive and offer unto God? Insomuch that by that time our tongue hath gotten them, our heart seemeth to have forgotten them, and so soon as our lips have once learned to deliver them roundly, our mind, resigning, as it were, her office, ceaseth any more to think of them earnestly. The consideration of which our fault and infirmity ought to stir us up to call upon God in humble prayer that whensoever we meet together to hear anything that concerneth His honor and our own duties He would vouchsafe us the favor of His good spirit, so that we may come with prepared wills, ears, and hearts, not slightly and formally to hear and conceive, but headily and substantially to weigh and work each man that which to his calling and duty appertaineth.

And therefore, inasmuch as order and the time have now brought us together to confer our labors upon such things as every man knoweth to appertain not only to the glory of God and the service of our prince but also to the common benefit of this our country [27] and to the particular good of us all, I trust you will use both such attention in hearing and such intention in doing of that which belongeth to your parts as the gravity of the causes themselves, the necessity of these evil times, and your bounden duties by oath now taken do require at your hands, not passing over the matter slightly because for the more part you have heard it often and do already know it, but rather entering so much the more carefully into the consideration and execution of each part thereof, as heretofore having heard much of it, yet hitherto you have done little or nothing that tendeth to the performance of this duty.

All men do see, and good men do behold it with grief of mind, that sin of all sorts swarmeth and that evildoers go on with all license and impunity. If the cause be searched for it shall never be found in the want of laws, for (God be thanked for it) sin in this age and light of the Gospel is not only detected by the mouth of the preacher but also prohibited by the authority of the prince. But (as the poet said well), *Quid leges sine moribus vanae pro-*

---

[27] *Country:* usually means, as here, a locality or neighborhood of no fixed boundaries, the area in which a man felt at home.

ficiunt? Quid tristes querimoniae, si non supplicio culpa recidi-tur? [28] What shall we do with laws without manners? And what shall we get by complaining of faults if they be not cut off by severity of punishment? The cause of this evil, no doubt, is originally in the mischievous minds of the offenders themselves, but yet secondarily and not finally in the remiss dealing of those persons that are put in trust with the execution of such laws as we have. And who those persons are I will make you yourselves judges of it.

Our good Queen is the supreme executioner of all her laws. Between her Highness and you, in this part of the law, stand we that are justices of her peace. Between us and the offenders are you set chiefly that be sworn to inquire of offenses. Her Majesty, as a good physician of the diseases of her country and people, doth continually for her part offer remedy and medicine for the same: sometimes in her leets, lawdays, and turns; sometimes in her commissions of oyer and determiner and gaol delivery; and many times by us in this her commission of the peace. And as it pleaseth her Highness to use us as the mouth of her laws in this behalf (for indeed we ought to be *lex loquens,* a speaking law), so also she appointeth you that be jurors in place of the eyes of the same law. But how shall we that be the mouth speak unless you the eyes will first show and tell us whereof? For as the physician will not give medicine until he understand the grief of his patient, the which also he can never perfectly do without his own report and telling, so neither can the laws, which are the very salves of our country sores, be discreetly applied by us without the aid of you or such as you are, who by reason of your manifold doings and dispersed dwellings in the shire abroad do not only see and understand but do also many times in your own persons taste and feel of the griefs of the same and are therefore specially chosen out to make report of them. Now therefore, if you seeing offenses do show them unto us, we will be accountant to her

[28] Horace, *Carminum,* iii, 24, 33–36, in reversed order of lines.

Majesty for the faults of our country if they be not amended. But in the meantime if you, seeing, either will not see at all or but see through your fingers, then must we require at your hands not only that fault of your own willful blindness but also all such other offenses as by your concealment do escape unpunished.

It is you that can see, if you will, the roots and first springs of all these evils that infest and trouble the country, and in you therefore chiefly it lieth to cut them off in the tender herb and before that they do grow to dangerous ripeness. For, if you would find out the disorders of alehouses, which for the most part be but nurseries of naughtiness, then neither should idle rogues and vagabonds find such relief and harborow as they have, neither should wanton youths have so ready means to feed their pleasures and fulfill their lusts, whereby, besides infinite other mischiefs, they nowadays do burden all the country with their misbegotten bastards. If you would complain of unlawful gaming in the day, of untimely walking in the night, and of unseemly appareling all the year, you should hew and cut in sunder the first steps, as it were, of those stairs which do lead up to pickery, theft, and robbing. If you would open your mouths against them that give and take liveries against the law,[29] your own burdens would be the easier and you should not need to open your purses so wide when subsidies, musters, or such other charges come upon you, in which you now carry all your own load and peradventure somewhat else to ease other men's men. If you would present the names of regraters, engrossers, forestallers, and transporters

[29] Royal proclamations on this subject appeared at intervals. Elizabeth had issued one in 1572 and found it necessary to issue another on April 19, 1583, forbidding "the unlawful retaining of multitude of unordinary servants, by liveries and otherwise," and citing a proclamation of 8 Edward IV, cap. 2, which orders "that no person . . . shall give any such livery or badge or retain any person other than his menial servant, officer, or learned man in the one law or the other, by writing, oath, or promise." Lambarde's further argument doubtless refers to the ability of great men to get their servants released from the payment of subsidies and other charges.

of victual, and the faults of such as neither keep assize of weight and measure nor use any moderation of price in selling of victual, then should not the poorer sort have so just cause to complain of great want and dearth in the midst of this so blessed and bountiful store and plenty. If you would discover such as either do compound for money with thieves that have robbed them or that will not detect their names, then both should all men travel by the ways with less peril and this country of ours should not be everywhere so infamously reproached with robberies. The like (if need were and time would suffer) might be said almost of all other offenses, the which of small seeds at the first wax in time to be great weeds by your too too long sufferance and forbearing.

It pleased the Queen's Highness this last year to send out her general and free pardon,[30] thereby not only forgiving us the most part of our offenses that are past but also giving us great cause to use better obedience for the time that is to come, if at the least we will not be accompted manifest abusers of that her so bountiful grace and mercy. And therefore, seeing that you are now much eased in your presentment, as being made able to wield and overcome offenses against the law the mass whereof was beforetime altogether unmovable, I pray you, heartily endeavor with us to pull them up as they rise and to keep them under in their first shooting, and then shall not our country be so annoyed with the grown stalks, spreading branches, and sour fruits that otherwise will spring of them. Be not afraid (as men in your place are wont to be) that your doings shall be disclosed, for if they be you shall not want help to have it severely avenged. And I give those clawbacks to understand that it hath been adjudged equal fault in the eye of our law to do an offense itself and to discover the proceeding of himself and his fellows against it. Again, be not deceived (as the most part of such inquirers are) with a false persuasion that you ought to present nothing but that only which is brought in bill ready to your hands. For your

[30] *Statutes of the Realm,* IV, pt. 1, pp. 698–702 (23 Eliz., cap. 16).

duty and oath is not only to take information but also to make inquiry of all such articles as shall be given you in charge. And therefore, forasmuch as you are a company collected out of many parts (as it were so many eyes put into one body) and are also all alike sworn and charged, you ought not only to hearken to other men but also to give information and credit each one to another.

Frame yourselves, therefore (in God's name), to do that which is now at this time no less lawfully than necessarily required at your hands. And whatsoever hath been the manner of men in your place heretofore, labor you, I pray you, by a diligent inquiry and faithful presentment to perform that which of right belongeth to the time, place, and persons that you do now occupy and represent, to the end that we, hearing by your reports the griefs of our country, may make application of that remedy which her Majesty hath put in our hands, so that by the mutual travail of you and us together the glory of God may be advanced, the service of her Highness may be furthered, sin suppressed, our country relieved, and you and we all in duty discharged.

WILLIAM LAMBARDE
[*signature in Anglo-Saxon characters*]

ဦ

Charge at the Sessions of the Peace
At Maidstone, 24 September 1583

If the wills and endeavors of you that be sworn were as ready bent to the furtherance of this service as the necessity to have it performed aright is great, the opportunity good, and the means every way full and sufficient, then should there need no words to whet your minds, and then should this little time that we have be well spent in doing, which otherwise is but half lost in talking, of that for which both you and we be come together.

Charges to Quarter Sessions

For whereas the due correction of faults resteth in two parts, namely, in the discovery of them, which belongeth to you, and in the determining upon them, which appertaineth to us; if you, which by this office ought to be the very eyes and spies of the country for bewraying offenses, did not negligently overpass a great many of them and willfully wink and shut your eyes at the rest, then neither should offenders go on with such impunity, nor this country be so grieved with their wrongs, nor you so justly burdened with the fault, nor we so well warranted to lay it to your charge. For although the causes that law hath submitted to the authority and jurisdiction of this court be both many in number and weighty in matter, yet be you assured that as on the one side both the greater part and weightier sort of them ought to be presented by you and are not to be sought out by us, so on the other side also scarcely is there any of them wherewith we may begin but that you also may and ought to bring the same before us. It is evident then that you of the jury be the principal instruments of this business, put in trust by the law to solicit and procure the glory of God and service of the Queen, the quiet of the good and correction of the bad, the stay of the rich and relief of the poor, the advancement of public profit and the restraint of injurious and private gain.

And therefore, if God be dishonored by the imps of Satan and enemies of right religion, if the Majesty of our gracious Queen be contemned in breach of her laws by unbridled persons, if unlawful buyers and sellers do move dearth in the midst of this blessed store and plenty, if by countenance of retainers against the law many amongst us do not only escape common charge but do also vex and overcrow their neighbors, if by disorders in alehouse keepers your children and servants be corrupted in manners, bastards be multiplied in parishes, thieves and rogues do swarm in the highways, the lawful pastimes of the land be abandoned, and dicing, cards, and bowling be set up in place, finally, if neither public officers do content themselves with their due and allowable fees nor private persons of any sort do contain themselves within their lawful bounds, but (as the poet said) *Fertur equis auriga, neque audit currus habenas*,[31] every man almost breaketh loose without fear of God, restraint of conscience, estimation of law, or regard of charity—if these things, I say, be thus, then you that are called hither from sundry parts of the shire and cannot therefore but see and know and are also sworn to bewray the authors of these evils, you, I say, are chiefly to be charged with it, and you above other are to answer unto God, the Queen's Majesty, and your country for the same. If in the midst of these evils we had far to seek for law and to find remedy for these enormities that do annoy us, oh, how justly might we complain and bemoan our estate! But now when law is not only brought home to our doors but also put, as it were, into our own hands, and yet scarcely any man found that will once move his finger to advance it, how unworthy possessors do we show ourselves of this inestimable benefit of ready, easy, and speedy justice! Every man, I know, will privately at home complain of things amiss and seem heartily to wish amendment, but when it cometh publicly to his lot to have both time, place, and power to open the grief, then will he rather suffer the sore to fester than to make us that be the physicians acquainted with it.

Truly, as no man is more afraid to find fault with another than he that knoweth himself faulty, so, seeing that little good is done by way of presentment here, it is to be thought that such as hitherto have been returned to serve their country were men more meet to be inquired of than to inquire of others. And I fear me that little or no good service will be done till we put that law in practice which willeth us to charge another jury to inquire of your concealments, for with such silence are men in your place wont to pass over offenses that they may rather seem to conspire

[31] Virgil, *Georgics*, i, 514: The charioteer is hurried away by the steeds, nor is the chariot heedful of the reins.

with evildoers against godliness and good manners than to come with prepared minds, as they ought, to have wicked men made good by punishment. For mine own part, so often as it shall happen me (unworthily) to occupy this place and to find things unamended, I cannot but, in zeal to our country that wanteth help, in piety towards you that undertake so great a charge, and in acquittal of myself and my masters here that be come to assist you, I cannot, I say, but earnestly call upon you to take heedful consideration of your bounden duties.

I pray you now, therefore, suffer not yourselves to be seduced by the evil example of such as have occupied that place before you, but enter into an earnest examination of your present duty, remembering that you be sworn, that is to say that you have called God to witness of your promise, and that even so, and none otherwise, you desire help at His hands in your necessities as you intend faithfully to perform that which you have vowed in His presence. Call to mind that it is the service of the Queen's Majesty which is put into your hands, with whom you ought to deal faithfully as well in regard of many other benefits as also in respect of this ready justice that you and we all enjoy by her. Consider that you represent the body of your natural country, which lieth now afflicted with many griefs and putteth you in trust to seek help for her. Weigh the danger and harm that may ensue if weeds be suffered to overgrow the corn, and think yourselves weeders sent into the cornfield of the commonwealth. Finally, determine to show yourselves such in deed as in this office you be called by name, *probos et legales homines,* good and lawful men, good in your own persons and ready to put the laws in execution against such as shall offend them. These things if you bear in mind, God shall be pleased with you, her Majesty shall be satisfied in your service, yourselves shall be safe from blame, and we all shall be glad on your behalfs.

W. Lambarde

Thus much beforehand shortly, because the time is not long and the articles of your charge be many and long. Now to the articles or points of your charge, in the delivery whereof, if I shall dissent from, etc.

꙯

A Charge Uttered at the Quarter Sessions of the Peace [32]

At Michaelmas 1585

It is a matter of no small weight, good neighbors and friends, for you and us to have the administration of country laws committed into our hands. For, as the laws themselves be the outward guides and masters of our lives and manners, and as the due execution of them requireth such a sovereignty of power as immediately belongeth to the prince alone, so, when any part thereof is delivered over by her Majesty unto us it importeth that there is a certain choice made of us, by which, for the opinion that is conceived of our integrity and virtue, we are made censors or judges of other men's doings, and instruments or hands to do the very office of our prince and sovereign.

Most needfully then it behooveth us to enter into this service with washed hands (as the proverb is), and with cleansed minds,

[32] The heading that Lambarde originally wrote for this charge was "A Charge prepared for the Quarter Sessions of the Peace, at Easter 1584." This he later altered (in different ink) to read as it is printed. The date at the end of the manuscript, April 23, 1584, the date of composition, must have been only a few days before the opening of the session, since Easter was April 18. Lambarde's rejoicing over the blessings of the peace under which they lived was more appropriate when he wrote the charge than when he uttered it seventeen months later, after the Queen was committed to war in support of the Dutch.

that we may both satisfy [33] that credit which is reposed in us and also promote justice itself, whereof for the time and place we are made the means. This thing shall we the better do if we may find ourselves furnished with these three special points that be generally requisite towards the conservation or execution of all laws whatsoever. The first is a knowledge to see and understand what things be good and to be followed, what other things be evil and to be eschewed; what persons are to be cherished, and what to be chastised. The second is an authority or power according to that knowledge to confirm the good in their well-doing and to reform the evil for their disobedience and excess. The last is a will or mind prompt and ready bent to do that which in knowledge we see, which by authority we may, and which of conscience and duty we ought to accomplish and perform. And albeit every of these three points are indifferently common, as well to us that sit here as to you that stand there, since we both have our several parts in this execution of the laws and justice, yet forasmuch as I am specially put in trust to speak to you, I will address my words accordingly.

Your authority then is apparently warranted, in that you be orderly called hither to make inquiry and presentment of such things as shall be given you in charge. Your knowledge also shall be thoroughly informed anon when the articles of your charge shall be unfolded before you. And therefore there is no cause that I either entreat of the one or anticipate the other of these, but only to spend that little time which is afforded in preparing you to come to this service with that readiness and alacrity of mind that is required towards the performance of so necessary and good a work. You are to consider, therefore, that many others be overpassed and that you be specially selected and taken apart to inquire and present the disorders and griefs of your country; so that there is expectation and hope conceived of you that you will show yourselves men meet to supply the rooms that ye possess—

[33] *Satisfy:* written above the underscored word *answer.*

zealous, I mean, of the welfare of your country; lovers of virtue; detesters of vice; ready to cut down disobedience with the edge of authority, as having a right eye upon justice itself without any sinister regard of friend or foe, kith or kin, great or small, high or low, rich or poor, if you shall find any of them to make head against the law and policy.

And to say the truth, whether you will respect the religion that we profess, the peace that we enjoy, or the prince under whom we serve, these present times do require the employment of such and of none other men. For first, although we live (God be thanked for it) in the glorious light of the truth and Gospel, yet for the most part our work[s] are full of darkness, falsehood, and lying. Although we profess obedience to God and the magistrates, yet we practice our own corrupt and rebellious lusts. Although continency of life, sobriety in apparel, moderation in meats and drinks, temperancy in pastimes, labor in our several callings, and equity in all our deeds and dealings be found in our books and be much sounded in our mouths; yet uncleanness of body, vanity of array, excess of drink, dissolute game, extreme idleness, and most foul and subtle shifts in each sort and trade of men are found throughout our ways and conversation, so that we have need of good men, as I said, to line and square our words and works together.

Again, there is no time so meet as is the time of peace to put wholesome laws in their due execution. How happy a peace this realm hath enjoyed, and that how long together, in these days of ours, we ourselves do best feel, our foreign neighbors peradventure do envy, and the like thereof have not our elders at any time before us so much as once seen or tasted. But what increase of good manners (which is the fruit of peace and the very end of laws) hath this so long and sweet peace engendered? Nay, rather hath not the cold and remiss handling of laws in these peaceful days of ours begotten the like dangerous disobedience and contempt that very war and hostility itself would have brought forth amongst us? For as in war the inflamed hearts and courages of men, not easily restrained by the bridle of law, do wax fierce and do openly break forth into many beastly and savage outrages which they ought not to do, so also in peace, on the one side, the dull and heavy dispositions of some (not pricked forward by the spur of law) do slothfully omit in manner whatsoever good thing is commanded, and on the other side, the subtle and greedy wits [34] of others (not corrected by the rod of law) do privily commit whatsoever evil thing is prohibited.[35] It is high time, therefore, for good men to look unto it, lest otherwise we lose all the benefit that peace doth proffer us.

Lastly, the times hath been when the nobility and commons of this realm have (with all humility and heart's desire) begged at the hands of their princes the continuation of their country laws and customs; and not prevailing so, they have armed themselves and have sought by force and with the adventure of their honors, goods, and lives to extort it from them. But we (God's name be blessed for it) do live in such a time and under such a prince as we need not to make suit, much less to move war, for our country laws and liberties. We have no cause to strive so much and so long about Magna Charta, the Great Charter of England, as it was called. For our prince hath therein already prevented us, so that not only the parts of that Great Charter but also many other laws and statutes no less fit and profitable for us than they are freely yielded unto us, and that not to be fetched afar off by us but sent home by her even to our own doors; not to be administered by foreign judges and spies but by our own

[34] *Wittes:* written above the underscored word *natures.*

[35] Lambarde here deletes the following passage, printed here because of its length and its interest: "For what great difference is there, I pray you, whether a man lose his goods by a strong hand or by a deceitful head, whether men be incontinent in the field or in the town, whether they be idle at home or abroad, insolent in the army or dissolute in the town or city? Since the fault of the offender is equal in both, and the hurt of the commonwealth, that is offended, is inferior in neither."

friends, familiars, and countrymen; neither yet left our liberty to be used or not but earnestly required and under strait pains enjoined to be put in ure [36] amongst us.

Now, therefore, seeing that you are placed in this office and have accepted the room of credit, seeing also that authority is already given and that understanding shall be forthwith delivered unto you, and seeing moreover that the time of religion, the time of peace, and the time of so gracious a reign do not only invite and allure but do also charge and press you to take and use this opportunity and advantage for putting your country laws in due administration and practice, there remaineth none other thing to the full accomplishment of this a most profitable and needful service but only that you bring willing minds of your own unto it, lest otherwise, whilst all other things do abound unto you, you be found faulty and wanting to yourselves.

Be not tied, therefore, to the evil precedents of such as have occupied the place before you, but think it your honor to have stepped before others in the doing of your duty. Depend not altogether upon that which others shall bring unto you, but examine your own knowledges, confer your own advices, and give credit each one to another of you. Have regard to the persons that ye represent, to the oath that you have taken, and to the duty that you owe to your country service. Set before your eyes the reward of due praise that will follow well-doing, and the deserved ignominy and pain that falleth upon the contrary. Apparel yourselves with integrity against love, hatred, and other evil affections of your own, and be armed with fortitude and constancy against the displeasures, threats, and terrors of other men. So shall you deal serviceably towards God and the Queen's Majesty, profitably for the commonwealth and your own country, safely for yourselves, and uprightly towards all other men.

23 April 1584
W. LAMBARDE

[36] *Ure:* use.

₡

For the Quarter Sessions after Easter
1586 [37]

It is very well known, good neighbors and friends, that for the better performance [38] of all our actions that bear any importance with them it is needful for us not only beforehand to deliberate carefully upon the body and substance of the thing itself that we take upon us but also circumspectly to cast the eyes of our mind upon the time, the place, the person, the occasion, the manner, and such other circumstances as do either lead, accompany, or follow the matter wherewith we intend to deal. And without this foresight and wariness it is most certain that either we shall defraud the business of that good help and furtherance which otherwise we might bring unto it, or else (which is a great deal worse) we shall so distemper the whole action itself that our labor shall be to loss and we ourselves shall do evil instead of good.

For this cause, considering that our present assembly is for the putting in execution of sundry laws that make much for the tranquillity and welfare of our country (a thing that we ought at all times to have in dutiful regard), and foreseeing that a right consideration of the circumstance of the present time and age wherein we live will add some earnest endeavor to this our attempt, I fear that I may justly seem either to have forgotten the place that I am appointed to occupy or to have done injury to the service that we are about, if (without using the advantage of this or some other good consideration) I should suddenly adven-

[37] Evidently the speech was delivered when England was at war. Easter was April 3 in 1586; spring quarter sessions that year met on April 12; see above, p. 43.

[38] *Performance:* written above the underscored word *executiō.*

ture upon the body of our business and break [39] into the points that belong unto your charge. And yet, nevertheless, assuring myself that you are beforehand thoroughly persuaded as well of the goodness of these laws themselves as also of the utility and profit that may be reaped by the heedful observation of them, since those two points are commonly from time to time inculked [40] and made to sound in your ears, I will only take that little time which may be spared without doing wrong to the rest of our business and employ it in perusing certain considerations of the present time which in mine opinion do invite us to a more diligent and careful administration of our country laws than heretofore hath been observed by us.

Tht first consideration of the present time may be drawn from the religion that we now profess, the which, as it is the undoubted truth that abhorreth falsehood, the clear shining light that chaseth away the deeds of darkness, and the very ransom of our souls from endless destruction, so it behooveth us all that will bear the name of so holy and chaste a profession as this is to be not hearers or talkers of the word only, not empty clouds without rain or moisture, not tinkling cymbals whose delight endeth with the noise, nor like men that have forgotten their faces which they saw in a glass; but to be and become the very same in work and deed that we desire to be called by name; but to be transformed and fashioned into that which we do hear and learn; but to fructify through the moisture of that heavenly dew and influence that we receive; and never to depart from that which we see in the glass and book of this truth of God. And this is required at our hands not only in our private lives and conversations at home but also (yea, and that principally) in the execution of such public charges as be laid upon us abroad; so as we may as well by our authorities root out the evil that

[39] *Break:* written above the underscored word *rushe.*
[40] *Inculked:* an old form of inculcated.

82

springeth in other men as (by the grace of God preventing our endeavors) avoid the mischief that lurketh within ourselves.

The next consideration of the present time may be borrowed from this most mild, moderate, and best-tempered government under which we now do live, the which (as we all see) not only permitteth unto us the free exercise of our country laws and liberties (a thing that hath heretofore cost blood and yet could not be enjoyed), but also proclaimeth them and provoketh us to a more vigilant use and severe administration of them. The laws, howsoever they be wisely invented and cunningly penned, yet if they be not countenanced with the cheerful look of the prince and furthered by the loving favor of those that have the chief places of authority under her, are but dead elements of themselves and can never work their effect by any the industry of us that be of the meaner sort in the magistracy. Much less shall they avail anything at all if the prince and nobility should run (as in former times it hath been seen) a quite contrary course against them. But now, whilst (God be therefore thanked) we have such a prince as is well pleased not only to rule others but also to suffer herself to be ruled by the laws of her land, and have withal such nobility and counselors of state as intend nothing more than that law and justice should bear the sway and strike the stroke amongst us—now, I say, if ever is the fit time and opportunity offered to put the laws in ure and with the edge of the sword and authority thereof to cut in sunder those offenses that work annoyance in our country.

The third consideration of the present time is taken from this late declination of our long-enjoyed peace and our present disposition towards war, the which, albeit her Majesty hath in great wisdom undertaken, both most justly in respect of the quarrel itself (which is the cause of God and His truth), and most necessarily in regard of her own estate (which is the safety of us all), yet nevertheless it must be confessed that this, as all other wars, will bring the wonted evils and companions of war and hostility with it. For now such men as have more valor in their bodies than virtue in their minds will think that all the labor lieth on their hands and will therefore grow insolent and boldly adventure upon the breach of laws in hope that (for the necessity that we have of their service) they may not only escape punishment but pass without controlment for it. Now will your sons and servants strive to draw their necks out of the yoke of due obedience. Now will loiterers and idle persons think themselves warranted to walk at their wills. Now will beastly drunkards and blasphemers vaunt that they be valiant and serviceable men. Yea, now will thieves and robbers take upon them as if they were the only soldiers of the world. And therefore, as there is never more need to use the bridle than when the horse sheereth,[41] so now (above all other times) it is necessary for us to take the bridle of the laws into our own hands, with the sha<rp   > whereof thes<e unruly> beasts may be holden in and mastered.

The last consideration of the time present resteth in this, that we are fallen into the last age and times of the world, wherein, as our Saviour Christ hath promised, we see it truly come to pass that sin and wickedness doth mightily abound. For what banks or walls of law be there at this day which the main streams and floods of sin of all sorts do not either break through or overflow, for the suppression whereof either we must daily grow in zeal of justice as they overgrow all number and measure, or else what other thing can we look for but that in the end a whole sea and inundation of sin and mischief shall come upon us and provoke God hastily to make an end of it, of us, and of the world together?

These be the <considerations   > from the present time which I thought meet to unfold before you, being of themselves no less weighty in matter than seasonable for the present business, howsoever they have been lightly run over by me that may

[41] *Sheereth:* sheers suddenly off in another direction; shies.

not borrow sufficient time for the better handling of them. Now, therefore, seeing that transgression of good laws groweth with the age and years of the world, and that the more because we are like to feel that force which the time of war can add unto it; seeing also that by the commodity of so gracious a Queen and temperate government we are both invited and animated to a bold and exact administration of law and justice; and seeing that the religion of God (which we bear in our mouths) teacheth, persuadeth, biddeth, and bindeth us to be at war with evildoers and to glorify God by our obedience to all the godly and just ordinances of our prince and country; let us, each man of us, carefully endeavor for his part to redeem this evil and ungracious time; let us beat down offenses with the stroke of the same laws against which they be committed; let us combine and join ourselves together to resist evildoers even as they conspire amongst themselves to do that which is unlawful for them; let not us be afraid to extend the arm of law against them whom we see so audacious that they be not afraid to violate law in the sight of us all; finally, let us not be afraid to cut off treasons, murders, witchcrafts, rapes, and other felonies that be the highest and top boughs, as it were, of this tree of transgression (which when we have done others will spring up and flourish in the place), but let us also hew in sunder the master roots and mores [42] of idleness, unlawful games, wasteful apparel, alehouse haunting, dissolute living, cony stealing, and all other lewd and deceitful practices, which, as they do send the sap of nourishment to the rest, so, being once stricken off, the whole tree, both in bough and body, will by little and little pine away and die together. This if we shall do, and you especially, upon whom the chief charge of this service now dependeth, then shall our time be so spent as God shall <have> the glory, <her> Majesty < > the quiet comfort and commodity by it.

[42] *Mores:* large roots.

Thus much generally for the better preparation of your minds towards this service. But now, that you may also particularly understand what belongeth to the execution of the same, I must, etc.[43]

ళ

Charge for Sessions of the Peace

1587

Amongst many things, good neighbors and friends, that for excellency in their use are most worthy to be maintained, I have not observed any one that is either more heavily gone about, more coldly handled, or more lightly passed over by us than this appointed service of God, our Queen, and country which for administration of law and justice the present turn and time of the year doth now bring about and offer unto us. For, howsoever each man of us be eagerly addicted to his own particular, so as no care is counted sufficient, no toil is taken to be enough, nor any cost or expense is thought to be too much or too great that is employed for the obtaining of our desires of that nature; yet whensoever it cometh to our lot to undertake anything for the common good and public benefit, so dull, so sparing and niggish are we found that we may justly be thought rather to be drawn unto it by others than to come of ourselves, rather to perform some custom than to discharge any conscience, and not so much to seek the correction of evildoers as to save and shun that penalty which for our absence might fall upon our own heads. And hereof it cometh that whilst we lull and rock ourselves asleep in this cradle of security, offenders of all sorts are exceedingly multiplied, recusants to serve God are daily more and

[43] Manuscript ends. Lambarde presumably began his formal charge at this point.

more indurate, disloyal subjects from time to time more dangerous and desperate, thieves and robbers do everywhere abound,
vagabonds and rogues do swarm abroad and flow over all, idleness reigneth, drunkenness braggeth, forbidden pastimes are
openly frequented, unlawful trades of life are freely haunted,
oppression wringeth many, covetousness catcheth all things, and
deceitfulness overreacheth all men. And what marvel is it, since
we that have the staff in our hand strike not, that have the power
of law committed unto us and use it not, that come as if we would
seek but find not, that do seem to inquire but present not; or if at
any time it happen that we discover and judge the fault, yet sel-
dom or never do we pursue and pay it with condign punishment.
If this way be still kept on and continued, what other thing may
we look for in the end but that in so working a sea of sin and
wretchedness as this age is the ship of this commonwealth shall
be in peril either to be dashed against the rocks or otherwise to
be lost and wrecked?

And therefore, whilst we have yet a most gracious and careful
prince and pilot sitting at the helm to direct us, whilst the wind
of inward peace and tranquillity bloweth so prosperously for us,
and whilst our shipping and tackle be yet strong and untorn, let
us agree to turn sailor and to bend our labors towards such a
course as neither her Majesty shall have cause to think this credit
evil bestowed upon us nor offenders against good laws shall have
any color to persuade themselves that we come hither but for
show only and that we will not or dare not board and set upon
them. There can be no greater argument, in mine opinion, to
convince us all of evil minds than that living in the midst of so
many transgressions, and having the free use of law in our own
hands, we extend it not against them.

For truly, if either we found not ourselves guilty of the selfsame offenses that we ought to punish in other men, or had any
regard of that weighty charge that is laid upon us, or carried any
fear of God, or nourished any love of religion and virtue, or

maintained any liking of the common good, why should we not draw the sword of authority [44] against offenders, and why should we not strike, hurt, wound, and (if the case require) kill and slay them with it? But I must contain myself, for albeit I heartily wish that this or any other speech of mine might whet the minds of us all and set a sharper edge upon us, yet, forasmuch as this present place calleth me to deal more specially with you of the inquiry, upon whom, to say the truth, the profit of this service chiefly dependeth, I will address my talk accordingly.

Those men teach not amiss, in my judgment, who, when they are desirous to instruct others how to do and to perform anything aright, do bestow their chief labor and travail in declaring what things they shall not do and what should be avoided and eschewed by them. For if that lesson be truly learned, then is the way to well-doing made plain and open by it. And therefore, as I have sundry times in this place showed the fair way that leadeth right to the discharge of the duty of such public inquirers as you are, so will I now at this time discover unto you some of those byways and bypaths that (if you take not heed) will seduce and mire you.

1. It hath been the common opinion of men in your place that they ought to present nothing unto the bench save that only which is given in evidence by others unto them. But this is a bypath, and therefore be not led out of your way with it. Your oath and duty is not only to hear and receive what others shall bring but also to inquire and present what yourselves do know. Every man of you hath sufficient credit to inform his fellow jurors; and seeing that you be all sworn and charged alike you ought to believe and credit each one another. You are a body gathered of diverse parts, dispersed throughout the shire (as if it were so many eyes put into one head) that nothing might escape your sight and knowledge. Close not your eyes, therefore,

[44] *Authority:* written above the underscored word *Lawe.*

but look abroad and wide open. So give trust to the faithful reports of other men that in the meantime you believe and trust yourselves before them all.

2.   Others have been well contented to make presentment but so far forth only as it touch not those men that be their betters and that will be angry and offended if they may know it. But take you heed, for this also is a bypath that leadeth to perjury. It is a part of judgment, good friends, that you have in hand, and in judgment, you know, there ought not to be regard or respect of persons. If any be afraid to offend for doubt of revenge, let him be afraid to offend God in perjury, that can and will surely be avenged of it. As for the anger of any mortal man, it cannot offer so grievous harm to your bodies or goods for the satisfying of his revengeful wrath as yourselves shall draw upon your own souls if you willfully run into this fault for fear of displeasing him.

3.   A third sort there is so loving and careful of their own friends that a man would think they came hither with none other mind but only to provide that nothing be presented which may be prejudicial or harmful unto them. But error is the end of this byway, and therefore enter not you into it. For these men never learned that, howsoever our kinsfolks, neighbors, and friends be dear unto us, yet the love of God and our country ought to be nearer and dearer than they all. And what manner of love or friendship is this, I pray you, either towards others, when we feed and soothe them in their faults, or towards ourselves, when by willful winking we make us partners of the selfsame offenses [45] that others have committed?

4.   But now, as all these be too slow of pace and do need the spur, so have I seen others so hasty and swift that it was more than need to cast a snaffle or bit upon them. These come as pressed soldiers, made out for none other end but only by presentment to revenge their own or other men's quarrels, and so

[45] *Offenses:* written above the underscored word *faultes.*

that they may thereby either satisfy their own private lusts or serve the other's turn, they care not what become of the rest of the common service. Let these also go alone without you, if they will go in this way that goeth to destruction. For, even as a furious fool that longeth to be revenged upon his enemy will not stick to run upon the point of sword, that he may give him a blow though it be but with his bare fist, and is slain for his labor, so these men do take revenge and wreak their malice not so much upon those whom they pursue in this mischievous hatred as upon themselves, their souls and consciences, when they achieve their desire by this abuse of their oath, office, and duty.

These be some of the bypaths whereof I thought fit thus shortly to forewarn you, that leaving them on either hand you may hold on that right, strait, and perfect way that cannot but bring you in the end to the full performance of the charge that we have laid and you have taken upon you.

Now, therefore, if neither you will suffer yourselves to be holden back with slothful negligence, nor to be blinded with sinister favor, nor to be driven out of your way by false and vain fear, nor to be spurred on with desire of injurious revenge, but shall go about this business with an even and steady pace, walking circumspectly in the Queen's high, broad, and beaten way, having God for your guide, using good conscience for your companion, taking the law for your just defense, and setting religion, equity, and honesty for the only butt, mark, and end of your whole travail, labor, and journey, then shall the honor of God be promoted, then shall her Majesty's service be advanced, then shall the country be much benefited, yourselves honestly acquitted, and we all made glad and well apaid by it.

And now, forasmuch as it sufficeth not to prepare your minds towards this service unless your knowledges be also informed for the execution of the same, I must descend to a particular enumeration of the points of your charge, the which, that I [46]

[46] Manuscript ends.

ช

At the Quarter Sessions after Easter
At Maidstone, 1588

There is no doubt, good neighbors and friends, but that naturally and without any help of persuasible or enticing speeches each man doth of himself earnestly affect that which in his own opinion he hath propounded to be good and profitable for him, and doth therewith bend and employ all the powers of his body and mind to achieve and win to the same. But yet, as all men do not join and agree in the opinion of that which they take to be good and profitable, so, itself being indeed but one and always the same (howsoever the minds of men be different and variable), it falleth out continually that to allure and draw men to a true liking and practice thereof no art of speech is found sufficient, no persuasion is forcible enough, nor any labor or pains can be too often iterate.

And hereof it is that on the one side the ambitious man cheerfully climbeth the steep and laborious ladder of preferment, the covetous person will forsake both food and rest to run after his gain and lucre, the haughty and cruel doth eagerly pursue his revenge, and each other dissolute body danceth joyfully after the pipe of his own sensuality, lust, and pleasure. But on the other side, to reduce men to the exercises of religion and virtue (the only good marks at which we ought to level and aim), *hoc opus, hic labor:* that, I say, is a world of work and business, and that needeth a most wise and cunning enchantment, so swift are our feet to follow that which under the appearance of good leadeth to destruction, and so lag, or rather lame, are we found in the way which only and truly is good and profitable to us.

And therefore the lawmakers of this land have from time to

time, and specially in this age of ours, most diligently labored to plant in the orchard of this commonwealth the very true sets of religion and virtue, that by the pleasant and sweet fruits thereof the glory of God might be enlarged, the renown of the realm might be advanced, our good prince, her Majesty, might receive the comfort, and we ourselves might reap and enjoy both the pleasure and profit of it. For the better effecting whereof also they have not only propounded sundry rewards for the good and pains for transgressors but have moreover appointed ordinary assemblies of officers, inquirers, judges, and justices, armed with sufficient credit, cunning, and power, for the seasonable digging and dunging of these plants, and for the convenient watering, cutting, pruning, and whatsoever needful husbandry of the same. And lest we should either be wearied in seeking these needful helps a great way off and far from us, or should be over-roughly entreated by strange persons that might be sent for the administration of them amongst us, the selfsame laws have brought justice home to our very doors and have commanded the same to be distributed by men of our own country, yea, our near neighbors and familiars, our dear friends and kindred.

But now, if in the midst of all this provident, careful, and kind circumspection these plants of piety and virtue do not fructify but are either covered with moss, eaten with canker, or overtopped with noisome briars, bushes, or trees; if instead of the true service of God that blockish superstition of the romish Antichrist do gather root; if in place of peaceable life, upright dealing, honest labor, seemly clothing, frugal diet, and allowable recreations there be everywhere found and seen violent and injurious actions, idle loitering, unruly gadding, excessive apparel, immoderate bibbing, forbidden pastimes, and generally vices of all sorts to bear the sway and to reign with full license and impunity, is not then the whole fault hereof to be imputed unto us, and are not we answerable to God, her Majesty, and our country for it?

Charges to Quarter Sessions

How all things be disordered abroad we all cannot but to our great grief and shame both see and sorrow, and what is ordinarily done for reformation here in this place is so soon told that two words and those, *almost nothing*, may comprehend it. For, besides those causes which we ourselves of the bench do bring from home with us, what receive we commonly from you that be sworn but *omnia bene*, when you might more truly complain *omnia pessime*, all is stark naught and out of joint. And for proof hereof I do refer to the consciences of those that accustomably do frequent this court and assembly whether there have been during all these ten whole years so many presentments yielded unto us as there be articles delivered to you at any one of these quarter sessions. If there have wanted matter, your predecessors are already excused, but if matter have abounded and the want hath been only in their minds, I beseech you that their fault be no longer followed. And if nothing shall be brought unto you by other men, yet shall it be right acceptable unto us if you shall present so much only as yourselves, of yourselves, do know to be offensive. So often as I deliberate with myself of some fit mean for remedy of this evil (so rooted by custom of long growth that it is hard to be pulled up, and so easy and plausible of itself that many will loathe to change it for a more painful and dangerous), I can think of none other way but that which law hath offered, namely, that we ourselves must both make choice of those that shall inquire for the body of the shire, and must withal impanel a second jury that (having vigilant eye upon the first) may offer presentment of all that which shall be concealed by them.

In the meanwhile, I am to hope better of you that be now called and sworn, whom I know not particularly to have offended in this behalf, and do therefore in that hope earnestly pray you that you will consider with yourselves that you ought not to come for custom only but for conscience chiefly; that you have now taken in hand the cause of God, whose sight cannot be bleared, the service of your prince, which ought not to be abused, and the cure of your country sores, that have great need to be healed by you; that this age of the Gospel requireth other manners and may not endure such corruptions; that this peaceable government (wherein we have long lived) affordeth a free and unfearful administration of law and justice; and, finally, that evil manners (if they be not cut off in the tender herb) will in time grow so proud and rank that too late and in vain you may repent you that you did not in good season lay the hook and hands unto it.

༄

Charge at the Quarter Sessions of the Peace At Maidstone, 24 September 1588 [47]

So often and ordinarily do we repair to this place and for this service, good neighbors and friends, that the end of our coming hither cannot but be understood to the meanest of all the assembly. And yet so little do we profit our country by this labor that it is no less expedient for us to recommend our action to the hearers at each time of our meeting together than if we propounded some strange matter whereof no man here had any foreknowledge at all. For if a man would, on the one side, call to remembrance how many most godly, politic, and wholesome laws be at every session published, with earnest exhortation and desire to have the same embraced and put in execution, and should also, on the other side, consider and behold how transgressions against those statutes do daily grow from evil to worse and are now mounted to an heaped and overflowing measure, so as, like evil humors, they threaten at the least some extreme sick-

[47] This speech was delivered scarcely a month after the defeat of the Spanish Armada. It is amazing that Lambarde makes no reference to it.

ness if not the utter decay and death of the body of this commonwealth, he shall be forced to think and confess that howsoever there be some at the bench that proclaim good laws, yet there come none to the bar that do give ear and willingly mark them.

It is not enough for us, good neighbors and friends, to present ourselves at the time and place appointed unless we come also with prepared minds to perform the service for which we are called. Neither will it serve the turn, though we mark well what is said and do mind to follow it in our own persons, unless we do therewithal endeavor to extend it to other men and by such means as we have compel them to the observation of that which is committed to our charge. The very end of law, as one said right well, is obedience, and the end of obedience is the life and safety of the commonwealth. And therefore (since we are public persons and have the credit to execute our country laws), if we shall come hither for show only, or for fashion's sake, and shall not both seek and ensue the amendment of manners and correction of misdoers, what do we else but wittingly betray the life of the commonwealth into the hands of such as lie in await to take it?

Whenas the common corruption of our nature is such that even the best men do many times fall and offend the good constitutions of their country, it cannot be chosen but that such as delight in wickedness and sin do exceedingly transgress, especially in these last days, which are evil, and in the days of war, which of all other be the worst. Some have thought it good policy to forbid their subjects all traffic with foreign nations, fearing that merchants would bring over from each place the vices of their own country with them. And have not our countrymen, think you, by their continual travel abroad transported unto us the evils of those nations with whom they have been conversant? Have not our most obstinate recusants and unnatural conspirators fetched their popish treason from beyond the seas? Have not

Italy and France sent us swarms of Jesuits and seminaries, that privily minister poison to our souls and stir up Spaniards with open hostility to invade the realm? Have not these Low Countries infected our people with drunkenness, which (as drunkards be always seditious) hath caused them to mutiny whilst they were for a time at home? And have not the same countries so trained up our soldiers in boot haling [48] there that many of them will do nothing but booty and rob when they return? These shortly be some of the wares that we receive from foreign countries, the fruits that are reaped in the harvest of war, and the faults of this last and worst age of the wicked world. Many others there be that do spring from the same fountains but not so proper to this present service, for which cause I spare to make rehearsal of them. Neither do I speak of these as utterly condemning all war and intercourse, for I acknowledge them both lawful, the one for necessity and the other for profit.

But this much I have said to this end, that as by these occasions evil doth continually increase and almost environ us on all sides, so you ought to be daily more and more careful and circumspect to apply those remedies which God, her Majesty, and the freedom of your country have vouchsafed, lest otherwise it come to pass that by your own negligence the mischief exceed your power and oppress you in the end. Lose not therefore, I pray you, the benefit of so precious a jewel as law is, being both brought home to your doors and committed into your own hands. Leave not your country worse conditioned to the posterity than you have received it from your elders. Have a conscience of your oath to God, a care of your allegiance to her Majesty, a love to your country, a will to comfort the good, and a zeal of godly justice that may either amend or make an end of the evil and bad.

[48] *Boot haling:* plundering.

ᴘ

Charge for Sessions of the Peace
April 1589

If our studies and endeavors about this service, good neighbors
and friends, were as prest and forward as the time of our coming
hither is ordinary, the necessity of our help is great, and the
authority that we have is both free and liberal, it could not but
in short time ensue that we should reap more joyful fruits of our
travail than we do, as well towards the advancement of the
service of God and her Majesty as also for the general amendment of evildoers and the particular quiet of every of ourselves.

For if we will consider the most ample and beneficial power
that the laws of our realm have, of very credit, committed to our
own administration and charge, spreading itself almost universally over those things that do either advance the religion of
God, maintain the estate of our Queen, or preserve our own both
public and private good and tranquillity, we shall be enforced to
acknowledge ourselves blessed above many, yea, above any other
nations, who need not to seek afar off to the physician of justice,
as they do,[49] but have ready, even in our own hands, the remedy
of almost whatsoever malady and disease that the wickedness
of this age or the weakness of our life may breed in any part of
our common body.

But now again, if casting our eyes about we shall discover manifold corruptions and noisome manners to run and reign amongst
us; if, I say, we may espy sundry that work the dishonor of God
by the obstinate withdrawing of themselves from His divine
service; if many be seen to violate the sacred peace of her Majesty by murders, robberies, thefts, riots, and affrays, mo to dis-

[49] Possibly an allusion to French local government.

turb the repose and quiet of her people by embracing of juries, maintaining of quarrels, bestowing of liveries, and busying themselves where they have not to meddle, and the most of all to overtake and trip their fellow subjects by usury, forestalling, and engrossing; by deceit of weight, measure, and price; by corruption of wares, extortion of fees, and infinite other perjurious, injurious, and wretched ways; if generally officers be found negligent of their places, private persons disobedient to such as have public charge, servants to take excessive wages and to waste the same inordinately again; if the pitiful poor do starve by want of charity and the stubborn idle stray at will for lack of due correction and chastisement; yea, if all these and such other things be not feigned of me but be everywhere seen, found, and felt of you and us all, where is then the fault of all this, I pray you, but only in them that do lock up the sword of justice which they have in their hands, choosing rather to let it rust in the scabbard than to be drawn (as it ought) and used for execution?

I will not bestow my labor to excuse ourselves that do sit here (for blanching becometh not the place that I do now unworthily sustain), but rather I must frankly confess that we neither make condign preparation for this service before we come together nor do afford it sufficient time and leisure when we be assembled for it. And yet, nevertheless, I have reason to lay to the charge of you that stand there the greater part of all this offense and misdemeanor. For even as no good building can be raised but upon a sure foundation laid before, so neither can there, for the most part, any hearing or determining of causes be had before us without an information or presentment first derived and drawn from you, so that for you to conceal offenses presentable within your charge is, as it were, to stop the course of the water at the head of the spring that it may never run through and come to be used. And therefore, if you will acquit yourselves in duty (as you ought) and be desirous to remove the note of this fault far from you (as I wish you should), then must you not only give heedful ear to the parts of your charge but must also make diligent inquiry and render faithful presentment of such things as you shall find amiss. It is no small privilege, good neighbors and friends, which the subject of this land enjoyeth, in that he is not to be judged but by his peers and men of his own condition, neither that by such as be of remote dwelling but even by those of the same shire and neighborhood where the matter doth arise, and then also, for the most part, before such justices as do inhabit there.

The which freedom, as it was dearly bought many years ago with great loss of English blood in those civil wars that were undertaken for it, and was devised in favor of the subjects, who before that time lay open to the malice of the revengeful accuser and to the cruelty of the foreign judge, so ought it not now to be abused by any our loose and careless administration of law and common justice, lest if it be once more taken away we shall neither with the spilling of our blood nor with the spense of our lives be able to recover and win it again.

I am now, therefore, in the name of us all here, to desire and pray you, and as well by that duty which you owe to her Majesty's service and by that oath which you have taken in the sight of God and presence of men, as also by that love which you carry towards the common good of your native country, to exhort and charge you that (all precedent of former neglect set aside) you will admit into your careful consideration these matters for which both you and we be come together; that you will not lose the advantage of this your great and special freedom; that you will not spare for any sinister love, fear, or other affection; and that you will not depend only upon that which other men shall bring unto you but that even as you be drawn out of sundry parts into one jury (as it were so many eyes into one body and head) so you will each man bring with him from home the knowledge of that which he findeth offensive, and (conferring your knowledges) you will all together consent and join in one good and serviceable mind, voice, and presentment.

᭐

Charge for the Peace
At Maidstone, 23 September 1589

Albeit the time that we allow unto ourselves for this service is so short (specially the days now inclining to shortness, and a good part of the day already spent) that hardly it sufficeth for the orderly dispatch of the one half of the affairs that are to be handled here, and although also I might seem to offer great wrong to all the rest of our business if I should stick long in the entry, as it were, and keep out those things which are more worthy to occupy the time that we have, yet, forasmuch as in all our actions concerning the commonwealth a diligent preparation ought to be used before we go in hand with them, and for that (if to any other, surely to this piece of service) [50] we commonly come not only not prepared to do the good that we ought but resolved to leap over the harms that we might remove, I think it right necessary to say somewhat, as well for the instruction of some and the reformation of others, as also for the admonition and putting of us all in mind to do that which is the very cause and motive of our coming hither. Wherein, nevertheless, I must so moderate and temper my speech that whilst I handle one thing I hinder not another, and whilst I prepare your minds for the service, I consume not [51] the time wherein it is to be performed. Shortly, therefore (for short I must be of ne-

[50] The position of the closing parenthesis, omitted by Lambarde, is conjectural.

[51] Lambarde first wrote "cutt not of," later underscored *cutt* and *of* and wrote *consume* above.

100

cessity), I will give you to know, first what the thing itself is whereupon your labor is to be employed, and then what your own part and office is for the accomplishment of the same.

The matter and subject of all your labor and travail at this time, in a few words, is directed to the honor of God, the service of our sovereign, and the tranquillity, peace, and common good of this shire, our native country. For, in that by these laws (the execution whereof is recommended to our care and your charge) conjuration, witchcraft, and sorcery be forbidden; in that the Pope (that witch of the world) with his masses, bulls, *Agnus Dei,* and with his sectaries (the seminaries and Jesuits) be chased out of the realm; in that buying and selling in the churchyard, with fighting and brawling in the churchyard or church, be chastised with pains; in that perjury and prophesying be not left unpunished—what other thing is there intended by it but only that, all impediments being removed, the right way to the service and glory of God may be prepared and laid open? Again, in that diligent repair to the church is required, reverent usage of the divine service and sacraments is enjoined, that godly preachers may not be disturbed in their exercise, and that good and religious schoolmasters alone are allowed, what other thing is sought than this only: that God may be served according to His word, that His word may have a free course and passage, and that both old and young may be instructed how to please God, as well in faith as in the fruits that come thereof. As touching our Queen and sovereign, the same laws (acknowledging her to be the immediate officer of God for our good) do first make way to the true obedience of her by removing all foreign authority, then they require that we speak nothing but honorably of her, and that we commit nothing that may by any means tend to the hurt of her sacred life or person, but that we be ready with all the powers of fortune, body, and mind that we have to serve her in God and God by her.

Now if we will likewise consider how these laws do regard

ourselves in our lives and actions one towards another, we shall find that not only murders, robberies, rapes, burglaries, and thefts of all sorts are severely punished by them, but also that extortions in officers, violence, deceit, and infinite other abuses, whether in public or private persons, have their condign rewards set down in the same. Furthermore, the duties in all degrees be here established: artificers, servants, and laborers be kept in order; prices of victuals and of things needful for life be not suffered to be enhanced without cause. Law is given that the ground be labored, that the benefits of the water and air be not destroyed, that even dealing in weight, measure, and contracts be observed, that moderation in meats, drinks, and apparel be kept and holden, and finally that (convenient disports [52] being allowed) the defense of the country be not neglected.

Thus have these laws provided for us in soul and body, in goods, lands, and credit, to the which I know not what thing besides may well be added, of the goodness or utility, pleasure or necessity whereof if I should attempt to entreat I know not either where to begin or when to make an end, and sure I am that if there be any man to whom these things do not by their only names sufficiently recommend themselves, upon him it will be lost time to bestow any ornament or labor of speech whatsoever.

And therefore I will now address my speech to you, who, as you have the credit to be in a degree the executioners of all these good laws, so behooveth it you to discharge your own parts therein, if at the least you do not envy to yourselves or to other men the good and benefit that will come of the same.

Your office lieth in two words, to inquire and present: to inquire, first of yourselves, by a strait examination of your own knowledges, then of other men, by a diligent hearkening to that which they will lawfully report touching any the offenses against these laws and statutes. This done, you must not conceal

[52] *Disports:* diversions.

but present, not keep to yourselves but bring to us the matters so conceived by you. And herein are you not now at liberty as you were before but stand fast tied and bound, as well by your duty to your prince and country as by your oath and attestation made before God, to every of which I denounce unto you that you must think yourselves answerable and accomptant for all the evils of our country that by your defaults shall not be redressed. But now, etc., etc.

℘

Uttered at the Michaelmas Sessions of the Peace At Maidstone, 28 September 1591, et 33 Elizabethae Reginae

It is very usual and almost ordinary with those that do occupy this place wherein I do now unworthily serve to labor with all earnesty and art in the commendation of those laws, for the execution of which they do sit and such inquests as you are called before them, thinking thereby to inflame the minds of the hearers with such a love of the same as may carry and transport them over all difficulties to the performance of that service which they desire at their hands. This manner and custom of theirs, I confess, is not only laudable in itself and forcible upon some hearers but drawn also and derived from great antiquity, even from the example of those most ancient justices in eyre, as they were called, whose authority then ceased when King Edward the Third began his reign.[53]

But forasmuch as one and the selfsame dish, howsoever it be good or dainty, serveth not always the appetites of all men,

[53] *Eirenarcha*, p. 405.

and experience hath informed me that the meat of that kind is but slippery and stayeth not so long time in the stomach as is meet for the making of good nourishment, I will for my part and for this season offer unto you of another sort, which, howsoever it may seem unpleasant to the taste, yet being well chewed and digested will work, I doubt not, to the benefit of the body of the commonwealth for which it is prepared and shall be set before you. And therefore, omitting to recommend the religion and justice of our laws, two things which by the only mention and naming of them do sufficiently commend themselves, and letting pass all rehearsal of the benefits that do ensue by the diligent observation of the same (the which if any man seeth not he is too too blind, and if he acknowledge not he is utterly froward and willful), I will only propound unto you that great fear, peril, and danger wherein we stand to have the benefit of this free and familiar use of our country laws (through our unreverent and careless handling of them) to be quite and clean removed and taken from us, than the which I know no loss (that of the religion of God only excepted) that may fall more heavy or hurtful unto us.

The law or policy of this realm of England, as it is a peculiar government, not borrowed of the imperial or Roman law (as be the laws of the most part of other Christian nations) but standing upon the highest reason, selected even for itself; so doth it in one special thing above any other most apparently vary from the usage of other countries: I mean in the manner of proceeding that we have by jurors, which our law calleth the judgment by peers or equals, and that as well in civil questions that do arise privately between man and man as also in criminal causes that lift up the head against the commonwealth, in the latter of which we are not, as other nations, to be accused or indicted at the pleasure or for the gain or malice of any one or a few men but by the oaths and consciences of the twelve at the least, and in either of which we enjoy this singular freedom and prerogative that we are not to be peremptorily sentenced by the mouth of the judge, as other peoples are, but by the oath and verdict of jurors that be our equals, and the same not strangers born but our own countrymen, not far dwelling but of the nearest neighborhood that we have. Now, what safety to the bodies and lives of us all, what peace and security to our goods, lands, and fortunes, what assurance and comfort to our minds when they be afflicted with the vexation of law is wrought and brought hereby they can better report that have seen the practice of both the sorts, and we that live under the one cannot but see and feel to our continual good and happiness. And truly, were this laudable policy of ours sincerely put in ure by good and lawful men thereto sworn as our law requireth, it would be a hard and almost impossible thing that either any offender should pass undetected and without his due pain, howsoever he should shroud himself for help and protection, or that any innocent and guiltless person should be injuriously oppressed, though the judges or justices themselves would lend their best assistance to it.

For, as on the one side you of the inquest are a body or company collected out of all the dispersed parts of the shire, as it were so many eyes put into one head or so many wits consenting in one tongue or presentment, than the which nothing can be invented more fit for the discovery of evildoers; so on the other side not the judges but you, nor you alone but also another jury after you, is to pass in manner upon each offense before that it be made ready for judgment, than the which no shield or target can be of better proof for the defense of innocency.

But even as there is no thing so good and sound in the first institution of it which by evil usage and unclean handling may not in time be corrupt and depraved, so by the careless and dissolute service of jurors and inquests it is now brought to pass, we see, that where by this excellent policy no offense could escape or lie undiscovered, there little or nothing at all is now brought to light and presented; where misdoers might with small labor be met withal and cut off in their way, there now they swarm with *sauf conduit*, as it were, and be ready to overrun us; where the law is nearest and brought home to our very doors, there is the fruit of law furthest off and most removed from us; and where we have the execution of law put into our own hands, authority, and power, there is it now less beneficial to us than if we were to crave, beg, and buy it with the uttermost charge, suit, and prayer. For, to speak the truth at once and plainly, as my place chargeth me to do, what is the service of our country like to be advanced by all the juries that be summoned hither? Take away the matters that we of the bench do bring hither with us and, in a manner, the sessions may be shut up so soon as the charge that we give you is at an end.

And this is the only true cause for which both the Parliament of the realm and the council of estate, seeing that this way by jury is not prosperous, have and do daily bethink them of other courses and have thereby worthily deprived us already of no small part of that liberty and freedom which the ages before us have enjoyed. For why did one statute erect the Court of Star Chamber and without any use of juries endow it with an ordinary jurisdiction over riots, retainers, maintenance, embraceries, and some other misdem[ean]ors but only upon this reason and pretense: that jurors in their countries either durst not or would not deal faithfully in the discovery of them? Why did another statute provide that a great sort of other offenses should, upon information made for the King, be heard and determined by the only discretion of the justices of peace, without any jury at all but only upon this ground that through the great favor and corruption of inquests they were not punished as by law they ought? And albeit that the same statute was shortly after resumed, because many men were deceitfully entrapped and injuriously condemned thereby, yet why have sundry other later statutes, one after another, referred the proceeding upon diverse faults to the discretion of the same justices again but only because the selfsame favor and corruption yet still reigneth and maketh the inquests to conceal offenders? Why, I pray you, are there continually in every Parliament so many popular actions given by which a number of promoters and informers, like flies that feed upon the sores of diseased cattle, do live and are maintained amongst us but only because it is necessary to have offenses punished, though jurors and inquests would never so fain wink and shut their eyes at them? But, to come yet nearer and to bring the matter to our own selves, why hath the Queen's Majesty and her Council now presently brought in amongst us (to our no less shame than charge) this new invention of provost marshal [54] to rake our rogues together but only because they are compelled thus to correct the slothfulness of jurors and inquests that will neither make presentment of constables or borsholders for not apprehending rogues as law hath enjoined them, nor yet discover the names of such foolish persons as under cloak of charity do give relief and alms to rogues when law forbiddeth them? Now truly, considering that not only every town and parish but also each borough and hamlet of houses with us hath a peculiar officer resident therein, whose authority in this part is equal with the power of the provost marshal, there is no doubt but that, if either such officers would do their duties, or if good inquests would present their omissions and defaults, we should be able of ourselves to rid us of all that vermin much sooner than could twenty provost marshals, were they never so diligent and well bestowed. The like whereof I could verify in the rest of these [55] things of which I have spoken if the time would give me leave to go through with them. But the day passeth and the rest of our business stayeth, and therefore I must be short and draw to an end.

[54] Cf. Edward P. Cheyney, *A History of England, from the Defeat of the Armada to the Death of Elizabeth* (New York, 1926), II, 247.

[55] *These:* or *those;* the key letter is blotted.

Thus you see how by the only default of jurors and inquests the native liberty and ancient preëminence of the English policy is already by little and little exceedingly shred off and diminished, very like also in short time to be utterly lost and taken from us if you lay not better hands and hold upon it. Which thing if it should happen in our days (as God forbid that it ever happen at all) we shall be condemned by all posterity to have been the most ungracious and base-minded age of men that have lived here since the general conquest of our nation and country.

Stand fast, therefore, stand fast, I say, in this liberty whereunto you are born and be inheritable. Show yourselves to have before your eyes a fear of God, a conscience of your oaths, an obedience to your prince, a love to your country, and an earnest desire to leave safe and sound to your children and offspring this inestimable jewel and precious patrimony of a most liberal, easy, and sure law which your forefathers, not without sweat and blood, have recovered and left to descend upon you. Be not witholden by any fear or favor, nor pricked forward by malice or revenge, nor seduced and misled by corruption of any kind. But go on forward and forthright, as law biddeth, as conscience moveth, as virtue persuadeth, and as the necessity of these evil days and times craveth at your hands. For so shall God be pleased and her Majesty satisfied, so shall the good prosper and the evil be weeded out, and so shall you appear no less beneficial to yourselves than good and profitable to the country that you serve.

℣

Charge for the Easter Quarter Sessions
of the Peace
4 April 1592

There is no doubt, good neighbors and friends, but that voluntarily and without any help of persuasible or enticing speeches each man doth of himself earnestly affect that which in his own opinion he hath propounded to be good and profitable for him, yea, and doth therewithal bend and employ the whole powers of his body and mind to achieve and win the same. But yet, as all men do not join and agree in the judgment of that which they take to be good and profitable, so, itself also being indeed but one and always the same (howsoever the minds of men be different and variable), it falleth out continually that to draw and allure men to a true liking and practice thereof no art of speech is found sufficient, nor persuasion is thought forcible enough, nor any labor or pains can be too often iterate and repeated.

And hereof it is that on the one side the ambitious man cheerfully climbeth the laborious stair of his own preferment, the covetous person will forsake both food and rest to follow his gain and lucre, the haughty and cruel doth continually thirst after [56] his desired revenge, and each other dissolute body doth joyfully dance after the pipe of his own sensuality, lust, and pleasure. But on the other side, to reclaim these and such other men to the constant exercises of religious and virtuous actions (the only marks whereat we ought to level and aim), *hoc opus,*

---

[56] The words *continually thirst after* are written above the underscored words *eagerly pursue.*

hic labor: that, I say, is a world of work and business, and that needeth a most wise and cunning enchantment, so swift are our feet to follow that which under the appearance of good leadeth to destruction, and so lazy, or rather lame, are we found in the way that only and truly bringeth us to that which is good and profitable for us.

And therefore the lawmakers of this land have from time to time, and chiefly in this age of ours, most carefully endeavored to plant in the orchard of this commonwealth the kindly sets of godliness and good manners, that by the pleasant and sweet fruits thereof the glory of God might be advanced, the renown of the realm might be spread abroad, our good prince, her Majesty, might receive the comfort, and we ourselves nevertheless enjoy both the pleasure and profit. And for the better affecting hereof also these laws have not only propounded sundry rewards for the good and pains for transgressors but have moreover appointed solemn assemblies of officers, jurors, and justicers armed with sufficient credit, power, and policy for the seasonable digging, watering, pruning, and whatsoever needful handling of the same. Yea, and lest we should either be wearied in seeking these needful helps a great way off and far from us, or should be over-roughly entreated by strange persons that might be sent hither for the administration of justice amongst us, the selfsame laws are brought home to our very doors and are put into our own hands to be distributed by each to other of us amongst ourselves.

But now, if in the midst of all this most provident, careful, and kind circumspection of law, these plants of piety and virtue do not fructify but are either covered with moss, eaten with canker, or overtopped with noisome bushes and trees; if instead of the true service of God that blockish superstition of the Roman Antichrist do gather root within the ground; if into the folds of shepherds there do secretly creep some of that wolvish generation of priests which will needs bear the name of Jesuits

110

or Saviourists when they be indeed the most furious firebrands, witches, wasters, and destroyers of all the world; if amongst loyal subjects there be suffered to lurk most impious and obstinate recusants that will afford both harborow and other help to these viperous enemies of our souls and country; if where peaceable life, upright dealing, honest labor, frugality in the use of foreign and homebred commodities together with allowable recreations ought to have the place, there riotous and injurious actions, fraudulent buying and selling, idle loitering, unruly gadding, excessive clothing, immoderate bibbing, unlawful pastimes, and generally sin of all sorts doth bear the sway and doth reign with all license and impunity—if this, I say, be thus, is not then the whole fault thereof justly and only to be imputed to ourselves, who either close our eyes that we may not see or, seeing, do neither satisfy the credit that is reposed in us, nor do use the arm of that power which we have received, nor do strike with the sword that is put naked and ready drawn into our hands?

Every man, I know, will privately at home complain of things amiss, and will seem heartily to wish amendment, *quid tristes queremoniae, si non supplicio culpa reciditur?* [57] But when it cometh publicly to his lot to have both opportunity and power to disclose the grief, then will he rather suffer the sore to fester within the body than to make us that be the physicians acquainted with it. Truly, as no man is more afraid to find fault with another than he that knoweth himself most faulty, so, considering how little good is from time to time wrought by way of presentment here, it is to be thought that many of those which have been heretofore returned inquirers to serve their country were men more meet to be inquired of than to inquire of others. For proof hereof I dare refer to the consciences of those that do accustomably frequent this court and assembly whether in any ten whole years they have seen so many presentments yielded

[57] Quoted earlier, p. 69.

unto us here as they have heard articles delivered unto you there at some one quarter session. Yea, with such silence are men in your place wont to pass over the huge heaps of offenses that they may seem rather to have conspired with evildoers against the good and tranquillity of the land than to have come with prepared minds to have wicked men made good by deserved punishment. For mine own part, so often as I shall unworthy occupy this place and shall find this fault unamended I may not choose but in zeal to our country that needeth our help, in piety of you that might undertake so great a charge, and in acquittal of myself and my masters here that do present themselves for your assistance, I may not, I say, but continually and earnestly call upon you to give more careful heed to that which both the necessity of this evil time requireth and the duty of the service itself expecteth at your hands.

Now therefore, suffer not yourselves, I pray you, to be seduced by the evil example of such as have occupied that place before you but enter into an earnest examination of your own present duties, remembering that you be sworn, which is as much as to say that you have called God to witness of your promise and that even so and none otherwise you desire help at His hands in your uttermost necessities as you now intend thoroughly to perform that which you have vowed in His presence. Call to mind that you have in hand the service of our sovereign, the Queen's Majesty, with whom you are bounden and ought to deal most faithfully, as well for conscience sake and for the respect of many great benefits that you enjoy by her ministry, as also in regard of this present favor of ready and speedy justice that you and we all do receive from her. Consider that you represent the body of your native country, which lieth now afflicted with many griefs and putteth you in trust to seek help and remedy for her. Weigh the great danger and harm that must needs ensue if you suffer weeds thus to overgrow the corn, and think yourselves weeders sent purposely into the cornfield of the commonwealth.

Finally, show yourselves such in deed as in this office you be called by name, *probos et legales homines,* good and lawful men, good in your own persons and ready to put your country laws in execution against such as have transgressed them. These few things if you bear in mind, God shall be pleased with you, her Majesty will be satisfied in your service, yourselves shall be saved from blame, and we all shall be no less glad on your behalves than willing both to think and report the best of all your doings.

℁

Charge for the Peace

At Maidstone, 24 April 1593

et 35 Elizabethae Reginae [58]

If light and superficial running over matters of the greatest moment might be allowed for good expedition and performance, then right well might you and we, good neighbors and friends, be thought to have acquitted our country duties, seeing that (besides sundry particular meetings for the services at large) we do four times in the year generally assemble ourselves with all the meet ceremonies of a solemn and judicial session. But forasmuch as the execution of justice, which is the only true cause of our coming together, resteth not in trifling show but in effectual proceeding, not in the concourse of jurors, ministers, and justices but in the correction of transgressors and comfort of well-doing, not in proclaiming the laws here at the bench but in a constant observation of them throughout the whole

[58] The manuscript of this charge is more heavily altered and interlined than that of any other. At some points it is virtually impossible to discern, in the welter of carets and deletions, what Lambarde's final intention was. The more serious difficulties are indicated in footnotes.

limit and pale of authority, therefore, I say, we and you are thereby found so far from performing our due parts in this behalf [that] the knowledge of that our fault might no longer be smothered at home but hath sought and found remedy on high at the hands of her Majesty her Court of Parliament.

For, if you remember, it was [59] this last year made known unto you all, and that too by [60] your own labor and pains, what imputation hath been made of great negligence in us touching these three special things following: first, for suffering the religious peace of the church to be violated and the estate of the land itself to be threatened with danger by a sort of elvish and obstinate recusants; secondly, for enduring so long together without any complaint, as it was [61] said, so many wretched oppressions by the means of purveyors; and lastly, for seeing our country to be overspread not only with unpunished swarms of idle rogues and of counterfeit soldiers but also with numbers of poor and weak but unpitied servitors, we ourselves having in the meanwhile law in our own hands sufficient for help in every of these cases and yet not moving our least finger towards the amendment or redress of them.

And truly, although in great wisdom these few enormities have been purposely singled out from the rest, being indeed of themselves so apparent as we have none excuse wherewith to cover our negligence, and being withal so dangerous to the commonwealth as it was not safe to suffer us to sleep any longer in our so great default, yet are there, no doubt, too too many other things within our like jurisdiction and power wherein we commit no less oversight than even in those few for which we were so specially taxed. For as these popelings and recusants that be of any havior and credit do by their backwardness both stay many at home that would come forward and do animate

[59] *Was:* in the manuscript the word is reduplicated by mistake.

[60] *By:* a deleting line passes through this word, but apparently by accident.

[61] *It:* it is possible that Lambarde intended this word to be deleted.

the enemies and traitors of the land that are abroad, and as these polling purveyors do no less dishonor her Majesty than oppress and grieve her good people, and as these runagate idlers do unworthily devour the bread of those honest poor and shamefully defraud the realm of that service wherein they are with great charge sent forth and employed, so be there not amongst us, trow you, a great many that, seeking counsel at the mouths [of] soothsayers and witches, do fly as fast to the devil as recusants do run from God? Be there not another sort that under the cover of their offices do poll and shave as near the skin as doth the most greedy and gnawing purveyor? Be there not night walkers and night hunters that in their generation may counterpoise the worst rogues and runagates that wander by the way? Be there not, moreover, servants that walk inordinately, artificers that work abusely,[62] and victualers that both keep and sell unlawfully? And finally, to the increasing of these and many other mischiefs, be there not constables and borsholders that to save their own labor do wink at all sorts of offenses? And be there not also, which is the worst of all, jurors and inquirers that do and will conceal whatsoever lieth most open and object to their own sight and understanding?

But what do I in such multitude of matter stand upon a few particulars, or why do I anticipate these things before their time? Give you good ear to the articles of your charges when they shall be opened unto you; mark well the number, weight, and variety of them; call your own consciences into examination what heaps of transgressions yourselves do know; compare them with the small handfuls of indictments that you do use to present; and then shall you with grief of mind perceive how much you undertake and how little is performed by you, how worthily you have been blamed for those few before and how justly you might be challenged for all the rest that do remain.

---

[62] *Abusely:* Lambarde may have intended to write *abusively* or *abusedly,* but the vowel following the *s* appears to be *e,* and no other letter can be made out between this and the *l.*

Certainly now it is more than time that you make these our lawful assemblies such as seem no longer to be for custom's sake but for conscience, not for show but for service, not to save your own fines or amercements but to discharge the duties of your calling to God, your prince, and your country. And forasmuch as now you undertake the office of seers and have the charge to disclose the griefs of the commonwealth, whereof yourselves, being members, must needs have a near touch and feeling, it behooveth you to enter into the business for which you are called with minds void of all fear that may discourage your hearts, void of malicious and revengeful desire that may carry and force you out of the way, and void of corrupt and partial affection that may dazzle and blind the eyes of your wisdom and judgment. In a word, therefore, consider that as you stand bounden to God by your oath and promise now presently taken, to her Majesty by your allegiance, to your country by nature, and to your neighbors and friends by love and society, so, having now the means in your own hands, and knowing that her Majesty and the Council do behold your doings, you ought with all reverent care, duty, and diligence to procure these good things that make no less for the glory of God and satisfaction of your prince than for the common good of the shire where you dwell and the particular benefit both of yourselves and every your fellow subjects.

W. L.

༃

Charge for the Peace

At Maidstone, 29 April 1595

That it is the very drift, mark, and end of all good laws and policies to cherish virtue and to chastise vice it doth well appear, not only to the mind by discourse of inward reason and conceit, but also to all outward show and proof indeed by continual practice and experience. For even as within the natural body of man medicine doth both sensibly purge and cast out the evil humors that they be no longer noisome, and doth therewithal confirm the vital parts that they may be enabled to do their best offices; so likewise in the politic body of the commonwealth laws have their apparent worth and effect, not only as curative medicines against wicked doers that either by their act or example or both do breed the dishonor of God and distemper of their country, but also as preservatives from all those and the like evils, as well by emboldening such as have charge of authority as by comforting the honest labors of all such as be working bees in the hive of the commonwealth. And forasmuch as all the duties of all men whether public or private do concern either the service of God, the obedience of their prince, or the mutual life and conversation of themselves one with another, therefore also the laws of this realm have propounded unto us meet rules and directions, not only for the external worship of God by the free use of His word and sacraments and for the lawful and loving obedience of the Queen's Majesty by a careful preservation of her person, a dutiful regard of her honor, and a vigilant conservation of her rights and preëminences, but also for the tranquillity and good peace of ourselves, by commanding on the one side security for our persons and possessions, fidelity in our contractings, and diligence in our several places and callings, and by forbidding on the other side all force, deceit, corruption, idleness, intemperance, and many other abuses wherewith if these good laws were not, our whole course and conversation should be disturbed and could be nothing else but a continual confusion, horror, and a living death, if I may so call it.

But now again, no more than medicines can avail the body if they be not received into the body, nor weapons can aught prevail in war if they be not drawn and used, no more, I say, can these laws, though never so politicly devised, bring unto us any good at all whilst they lie shut up in our books only as dumb letters and dead elements, unless they shall be drawn forth and carefully put in continual ure and practice, which are the only means by which their sweet and wholesome juice, power, and virtue may be drawn and had from them. And therefore, most injurious and execrable is the fault of all those men that, either having the execution of laws put into their hands do not extend the same, or that otherwise do oppose themselves as bars and impeachments whereby the ministers of the laws may not do that which both the ministers would and their places of charge do require at their hands. For to such men we may rightly impute the whole blame and reproach that neither God is rightly served, nor her Majesty worthily obeyed, nor the common good of the country sought for and procured with such care and endeavor as appertaineth. Yea, we may in a manner repute them to be the very authors and causers of all the disorder, malady, and mischief that is bred and nourished within the body of the common-wealth amongst us.

But considering that by nature we are all very unwilling and loath to be charged with fault, and much more unready to agnize [63] or confess it, and for that also it is the chief part of our present business here to inquire, search, and sift out faults and offenses, let us, I pray you, examine where and in whom resteth this great fault that these good and beneficial laws be not executed, to the end that the place and part effected being thereby known we may accordingly find out and apply fit remedy and medicine for it. And herein I see no cause why we need either to seek far or to labor long.

For it is undoubtedly true that you and we have in our own hands, committed unto us of great favor and trust, the free administration and power of so many and so excellent laws as may suffice for the happy and full peace and profit of all the

[63] *Agnize:* recognize.

sorts of us, if the same were duly dealt and observed. We ourselves, I say, have this whole power in our own hands, you for information by inquiry and we for determination by hearing, judgment, and execution. So that necessarily between you and us lieth this grievous fault that the laws have not their due honor and desired effect. But whether more in you or us let that appear by this that followeth.

It must needs be confessed that without search and inquiry offenses against law are not discovered, without discovery they are not informed, without information they cannot be heard, without hearing they ought not to be judged, and without judgment they neither may nor can be lawfully and condignly punished. So that, take away discovery of faults by search and inquiry, which is the first motive and leading link of all this chain, and then must you necessarily therewithal take away and withdraw all the means, power, and possibility to deliver that good and profit which otherwise these laws do offer and we all might enjoy by them. Now, that you yourselves be the inquirers, seers, and searchers by whom we are to take the whole light and information of things amiss, the form of your oath, the articles of your charge, that special employment of you, and the whole frame and order of all this solemn proceeding do most evidently prove and convince it.

And therefore before such time as I enter into the points of your wonted charge I must specially recommend this one unto you as a principal article of your charge and inquiry: namely, that first of all you search and inquire whether you yourselves, that should present before our eyes the names and doings of these offenders, be not the greatest let and impediment that we cannot come to the light and sight of them. The fault is often and openly found, not only by us at these services of the peace, to our own particular grief, but also by the foreign justices in their delivery of the gaol, to the general reproach of our whole country, that neither our juries for inquiry do contain themselves within their known and prescribed bounds nor our jurors for trial of life will give ear, as they ought, to the matter of their evidence. For many of our grand jurymen, not content to be inquirers only as their office affordeth, will needs become justices both of *nisi prius* and of gaol delivery. And likewise our jurors for trial will not bind themselves to common law and the strict point of their issue but will usurp upon the office both of the chancellor and prince also. In that inquirers do not hearken only to such credible persons as upon oath do offer their bills for the Queen, but will also admit and hear the offenders that are to be charged thereby, what else do they, I pray you, but play the justices of *nisi prius* by such holding a plea and trying an issue where none at all is joined before them? And in that they will not give credit to honest and substantial persons directly sworn but do willfully extinguish the light of faults clearly proved unto them, do they not make themselves more than justices of gaol delivery, taking thus upon them to rid the gaol before it be perused? Again, in that our jurors for trial will needs moderate their verdict by a feigned equity and thereby acquit most guilty offenders, do they not also arrogate unto themselves both the office of the chancellor and the prerogative of her Majesty to whom only it belongeth to grant pardon to malefactors? I am not willing to make odious rehearsal of particular examples in this kind, though easily I could produce more than a good many; but I will rather sum up the evils that follow of this disorder and set you down the remedy for them.

First, good and well-meaning witnesses have not their due and deserved credit but are most injuriously discountenanced hereby. Then, law is shouldered out of her right course to the hurt of the commonwealth and grief of good men. And lastly, evildoers are not only emboldened by such impunity but are also many times armed with matter of action in law against such as have worthily brought them to their trial, a mischief of all others most mischievous and intolerable, that the wicked ones should not only escape the sword but therewithal strike and wound the good and well-disposed. The remedy of all which is to be found chiefly in yourselves and yet somewhat in us also.

To you it belongeth to present all that which either yourselves do know or which other credible persons do inform upon their oath, whom also you must take for credible unless you know them to have been perjured. For they may not be rejected by you because you see them grieved and offended, seeing that not they but the Queen's Majesty's self is the very proper party between whom and the offender any honest subject, howsoever offended, is a competent witness whereupon you may and ought to ground your presentment. To you it belongeth only to inquire and present, not to hear and determine, not to absolve or convince, and therefore also not to hold plea nor to admit the offender and his proofs. For all your doing is but only to inform the court, whereunto the party, being called, may offer his traverse,[64] and then, and not before, shall he be heard and tried, and that also not by you but by another several jury. Lastly, to you it belongeth to level your presentments and verdicts by the straight line of law itself without any fond imagination of equity or mercy, knowing that mercy lieth not in your mouths but either in the power of the justices that can give allowance of clergy or in the hands of her Majesty that only can make good her gracious and free pardon.

To us on the other side belongeth the correction of your misdemeanor and, by hearing the evidence to be openly given in court and seeing into your fault, either to bind you to appear before the lords in the Star Chamber or otherwise to charge another jury to inquire of your willful concealment and, that discovered, to proceed by fine and ransom to the punishment of you. And for the avoiding of all future inconveniences and better instruction of men in your place we have also thought it to

---

[64] *Traverse:* a legal term meaning the formal denial, in pleading, of a matter of fact alleged by the other side; a plea consisting of this denial.

belong unto us to leave with you from time to time some few and short directions against the which if any shall willfully offend we are resolved, upon complaint thereof, that we also will publicly hear the evidence and judge of their undutiful demeanor.

Thus much but by occasion of such only as heretofore have willingly run astray. For as touching the persons of you that be now presently called and sworn I have not to mislike but do hope well of your dutiful endeavors and do verily trust that you come prepared with minds desirous to perform that which belongeth to your charge. And therefore, that I be not overlong, I pray you in a few words to remember that as you are by birth all or the most part of one same country, by habitation neighbors, by special choice at this time visitors and inquirers, and by your present oath and office made answerable to God, your prince, and country laws, so it behooveth you to have a care of your native country, a consideration of those with whom you live and converse, a regard of your serviceable calling, a conscience of your oath, and a fear to fall into that peril and punishment which deservedly belongeth to those that offend in the duties of most weighty charge and importance. It is neither the fear of some nor the favor of others nor the love of yourselves that ought to withhold or restrain you. But you must heedily cast your eyes to and fro as men willing to search, that searching you may find, and finding you may present unto us the griefs of our country, our common nurse and good mother, to the end that by the mutual studies and labors of you and us together we may all reap and enjoy the sweet fruit of the law, which, as I said at the first, is to have transgressions corrected and to see religion, honesty, and good manners set up and advanced.

ᴇ

For the Quarter Sessions
20 April 1596, at Maidstone

Such is the condition of civil justice and politic government
that if it may find any exercise or motion at all and may be suffered to creep, as it were, and to crawl forward never so little,
yet it will not fail to bud forth and spread abroad most beneficial
and comfortable effects amongst them that shall give it enter-
tainment.

And truly, if the trial hereof were to be sought, the same might
be found amongst us here most evident and approved. For albeit that we neither assemble for justice so often as we ought
nor do make our meetings so much for service as for show and
fashion's sake, yea, though we inquire as if we would not find,
though we present as men not willing to accuse, and though we
judge and determine as if we sought neither to put down offenders nor to put any end to offenses, yet nevertheless even this loose
and careless administration of ours wanteth not some good
blessing and success amongst us. For hereby now and then
either a felon is discovered, or an incontinent person is brought
into question, or a turbulent peacebreaker hath his hands
bounden, or a lurking recusant is enforced to come forth and
make semblance, or a greedy oppressor is encountered in the
desire of his wicked will, so as it cometh to pass that we be not
altogether destroyed by murtherers, spoiled by thieves, vexed
by barrators, nor so overtopped by such other vile and most
noisome weeds but that we do live and grow, after a sort, under
the favor of this our cold and slack justice, though nothing so
well and happily as we might, yet far more calmly and defensed

than otherwise these enemies of God and good manners would afford us.

But if we could truly foresee and behold in our minds what heaps of happiness and treasures of blissful life would befall us if we did seriously attend this distribution of law and justice that we have in our hands, and could consider how much the service of God would be advanced, how greatly the obedience to her Majesty would increase, and how plenteously these good laws would fructify in all persons both public and private, old and young, rich, mean, and poor, and that as well in each branch and private family as throughout the main body of the commonwealth, oh, what incredible love thereof would the same then stir up within us! With what ardent affection and desire should we be drawn to pursue it, and how effectually would we labor to put it in daily ure and constant execution!

The law may not unaptly be resembled to an artificial organ or instrument of music which is prepared with tuneable pipes of all sorts and proportions and which by the help of the bellows and the hand of the organist or player will yield most pleasing and delightful harmony. For the Parliaments, being the common council of the realm, have from time to time devised laws most fit and tuneable for all the degrees of persons living under the obedience thereof, and those also are inspired and blown with the assenting authority of the prince, who desireth nothing more than to satisfy her people with the sweet sounds and strokes of her royal justice. But even as the organ, whilst it is only filled with the wind of the bellows and is not touched upon the keys by the hand of a skillful musician, affordeth no melody at all but only a confused noise and rude whistling, so likewise the laws, howsoever prudently ordained by conference of the wisest or strongly established by authority of the highest, yet if they want the hand and fingering of good and well-disposed executioners they do but buzz in our ears and they make no melodious or harmonical justice amongst us; howbeit the fault is neither in the laws, which are good of themselves, nor in the prince, which is the head and life of them, but wholly and altogether in them to whose hands and fingering the use of this so noble and necessary an instrument of a good and happy commonwealth is committed. And therefore, seeing that the distribution of our country laws is in great favor put into the hands of you and us, our parts and duty it is so to order and move the same that they may sound out and speak to all, not confusedly and without delight, but melodiously and so as it may be pleasing to God's will, answerable to her Majesty's desire, joyful to the hearts of others, and comfortable to our own consciences.

Many things, I wot well, there are which offer jar and discord in this our musical proceeding: as fear in some, favor in others, diverse affections in a great many, and the tract [65] of an idle and evil custom in the most of us all. But yet nothing that I have hitherto observed hindereth the service more than a sinister persuasion which many serving in your place have conceived in two special points: fantasying, by the one, that they be not only presenters but triers also of the causes brought before them, so as in their opinion their indictment is not only an accusation or charge but a very determination and judgment final against the offenders; and making, by the other, a conscience unto themselves not to believe whatsoever proceedeth by complaint under the oath of any person that is immediately grieved or offended, for that they presuppose it to come of malice or displeasure and therefore not to be admitted by them. But the one and the other of these erroneous opinions must be removed from you as being no less dangerous to the oath that you have taken than injurious to the service wherein you are employed.

Touching the first, therefore, all experience openeth unto you that your office is not to try but to present, and that your presentment is but a preferment or recommendation of another man's

[65] *Tract:* used in the old sense of "force."

complaint to the bench, the trial of the truth whereof is not submitted to you but reserved for another jury till the hearing of the traverse, if the offender will offer any. So that it belongeth not to you to hear the offender nor to admit his proofs, but only to weigh the complaint and the justification thereof upon oath, and so to examine the parts and circumstances of the same that no fraud lie hidden nor escape you undiscovered. But if you were triers indeed, then should the offender's mouth be stopped by your presentment, neither should he be received to traverse that which is found by you, the very contrary whereof is both daily seen and lawfully permitted. Be you not, therefore, willingly deceived by confounding in your opinion those things together which be in their own nature distinct and separate. For, in a word, all your doing is no more but as if you said, such a man hath complained of such an injury or violence done unto him, the trial whereof we recommend to you at the bench, ourselves seeing none impediment why it should not be presented by us as it hath been exhibited by him.

Now for the latter point, considering that in these days of ours hardly any man is found that will inform against offenders, either for the love of virtue or for the good of others but only for the relief of himself and to be revenged upon some adversary, so much the more ought your ears to be open to all such as do complain, lest otherwise, whilst the most men will not speak at all and the rest cannot be heard when they speak, the evil and wicked sort be permitted to hold on their full course and career without any restraint or controlment. The law of the land affordeth a writ to call his adversary, and heareth each man's complaint, without any oath, in whatsoever civil and his own private cause, and will not you receive a man's complaint upon oath in a case that is both public and criminal? Be you assured that if you will not admit complaints, you refuse to present, which is the ordinary mean and way to trial, and without trial it becometh not us to judge, much less is it lawful for us to correct or punish. And so consequently, as far as in you lieth you forestall and close up the way to justice, and withal you set open a gate by which offenders may on heaps throng out and escape unpunished.

Thus much only for this time of these two conceits that commonly seduce such as serve where you stand, with which I must conclude my speech, foreseeing that without injury to the assembly and service I may not misspend the time. And therefore, considering that your oath and charge is to inquire and present (which proceedeth partly by your own knowledge, but principally by the information of others upon their oaths), it belongeth to you neither to keep the counsel of such as offend the law nor yet to reject the oath of any man whom law holdeth for credible and which also giveth credit to each man that hath not beforetime been lawfully discredited. The rest of the blocks in your way, of which I spake, as fear, favor, and suchlike, are apparently evil of themselves and be therefore the more easily to be foreseen and avoided by you. But these against the which I have now specially directed my talk do creep in under a veil and cloak of conscience to do well, and ought therefore to be so much the more heeded and carefully shunned of you, the which if you will do, as I heartily pray you to do, then doubt you not but that you shall make two good and large steps in this journey towards good service, whereby both yourselves now and others that shall hereafter take the place may be encouraged to go forwards without ceasing until that you and they shall have finished the duties of your charge, both for the common good of your country and for the particular satisfaction of your own oaths and calling.

ၲ

For the Quarter Sessions of the Peace At Maidstone, 28 September 1596

It is an ancient truth, confirmed as well by the judgment of the learned that have written concerning the government of countries and commonwealths as also by the continual practice of all societies and nations, that even as no man can live comfortably without the fellowship of men, so no fellowship can stand without law and discipline; and that even as the body of man and all the parts and members thereof derive their life, sense, and moving from the soul or spirit of man, so the laws of each country and kingdom be the very soul and life thereof, by whose continuance they do joy, grow, and flourish, and by the neglect and want whereof they fall to jar, poverty, ruin, and desolation in the end. It is likewise most assured that laws be ordained, not to be read and published only, but also, and that chiefly, to be administered and put in execution, to the end that men may direct the steps of their conversation according to the right rule and prescript of them, knowing that as obedience is the end of the law, so the safety of the people is the end of that obedience. And hereupon, therefore, it hath evermore been resolved that such and so great is the use and necessity of law as that without it neither any private family nor town nor city nor nation nor the universality of mankind nor the nature of things created nor this mighty mass of the world itself is able to stand and continue, and that to take from men the exercise of law were to draw the benefit of the sun from the world, whereof palpable darkness, confusion, and horror of all things would immediately follow and fall upon it.

Now if the administration of law and justice be at all times so necessary and profitable, how should not the same be most be-hooveful and available in the tempests and storms of the commonwealth, when men are either terrified by outward wars or torn and rent in sunder by inward dissension or pinched and bitten by scarcity and want of things most needful for their life? For if wars do assail, then do so many perils beset the good that hardly they dare peep out and show themselves, and so many hopes do allure the bad that they break in sunder all the bands, not only of the laws of men but also of God and of nature and humanity itself. If dissension shall fortune to arise, especially for matter of religion, then is the conscience exceedingly shaken, and without conscience nothing can be sincere but all infidelity will possess the heart, so as both the religion of God and commandment of the prince shall be had in detestation, and foreign shifts shall be sought for, even to the betraying of friends, kinsfolks, king, and country. If scarcity and dearth be sent amongst men, then such as have any store do make their advantage without charity and such as feel want do murmur and mutiny, without all respect either of God that is the author of it or of their own sin and wickedness for punishment whereof it is laid upon them. And therefore, as in the more dangerous and working seas there is more need of vigilant pilots, so in these and the like troublesome seasons of the estate there ought to be most diligent care taken for observation of the laws, by the good or evil steerage whereof the ship of the commonwealth is either to be sunk or saved.

Now that we have been a long while together tossed in the waves of war, dearth, and dissension, there is no man so simple but he seeth, no man so safe but he partly feeleth, nor so hard and stony but he sometimes melteth to behold the long train of innumerable evil manners that are stert [66] up and grown by them. For since the time that our nation hath conversed with

---

[66] *Stert:* this archaic past participle of *start* survived into the seventeenth century.

foreign people in the wars abroad, what Frenchman so garish and light in apparel, what Dutchman so daily drunken and given to the pot, what Irish more idle and thievishly disposed, what Scot more cowardly, sudden, and ready to stab, what Spaniard more insolent, fleshly, or blasphemous than be a many of our own English, who have not only learned and transported hither all these vices of those other men, but are grown so perniciously cunning therein that they excel their teachers and teach it to others at home! Again, since that adversary, the man of Rome, first sowed the cockle of his excommunication in the hearts of our Catholics, how many traps have there been laid for the life of the Queen's Majesty, how many treasons have there been contrived for the conquest of the realm, what hopes have there been and yet are nourished of the Spanish invasion, what downfalls of natural duty and revolts from due obedience have we seen discovered amongst us! Lastly, during these last three years' dearth of corn and victual, what frauds have been practiced for enhancing of the prices, what bargaining in privy corners, what engrossing in open markets, what vent of foul and unwholesome grain, what coveting of good store, what conveying out of the shire, what multitudes of unlicensed alehouses be daily raised, what abundance of barley is continually malted, what excessive strong drinks be yet still brewed, how licentiously is flesh devoured, how obstinately is starch yet continued, and how many other wastes are now in this penury committed which even in the greatest plenty were not to be abiden and suffered by us!

I do not labor (as you may well see) either to feign things which be not at all, or to aggravate or make them worse than they be indeed; for it is work sufficient, and too much, only to recount the infinite swarms of evils that of latter years (more than in former ages) have invaded the realm and overrun it. And is it not yet time, think you, for the laws to awaken, and for the executioners of the law to look about them? Shall we yet still assemble and make our sessions for the only reading and publishing of our laws, and shall we not unsheathe the sword of authority and use it against offenders? We are not a little bounden to our predecessors for the ordaining of these so many good and beneficial laws as may suffice to a peaceable, joyful, and plenteous life; and I would to God that our posterity might find cause to thank us for the fruit which should descend by our careful execution and practice of them. If the commonwealth suffer wreck by these tempests whereof I spake, the blame must be theirs that, sitting at the helm, do not foresee the danger or, seeing, do not apply their endeavors to prevent it.

Concerning ourselves that sit here, I confess that as private persons we see all these evils even as all other men do, but as public officers we must see them by the relation of you who are to that end first dispersedly bestowed in office where you may best see, and then called forth, and now all together sworn to bewray what you have seen. If you will say nothing, it is not because you cannot find, for such is the number and variety of lawbreakers of all sorts and in all corners, that though you seek not them, as you ought, yet will they present themselves and find out you wheresoever you be come. But, on the other side, if you see and dare not speak, then woeful is your case, in that you fear not God so much as men. And yet, since that fear is the very root of all this silence and evil service, I will in two words tell a ready medicine against the fear of men. Spare none, but present all that do offend, and none will be offended with your presentments. For even hence springeth all displeasure, that being appointed the ministers of law you do not conform your minds to the image and likeness of law, whose condition it is to be all one, alike, and the same to all men, and which can neither be bowed by favor, nor be broken by force, nor be incited by malice, nor be corrupted by money or gift whatsoever.

Thus have you shortly heard me to run over as well the commodity of laws and the benefit of the execution thereof as also the necessity that your country hath and the present help and remedy that yourselves do carry in your own hands. Seeing, therefore, you be called hither, as I said, not so much to hear the laws opened only as to join with us in the execution of them, not for custom but for service sake, nor to serve the time but the truth, it belongeth to you to quit yourselves the best that you may of this blame which hitherto hath bee[n] worthily laid to the charge of men in your place and, performing your own parts by diligent inquiry and faithful presentment, spare not to lay and leave the rest of the service upon us, who, if we shall not accomplish that duty which remaineth, we shall not only be convinced in our own consciences of great infidelity to our Queen and country but shall also alone sustain the uttermost imputation of the same so great and grievous an offense.

༜

For the Quarter Session of the Peace

after Easter *1598*

At Maidstone

It may most truly be affirmed, good neighbors and friends, that in all actions of duty and charge the care and consideration of such as undertake the same ought to equal and counterpoise the weight of the business themselves, so as always in causes of the greater moment greater heed and advisement ought to be taken and applied by us. This considered, I see not how, after this proportion, we here can be sufficiently careful for the administration of our country laws which we are now by orderly revolution of time to take upon us, knowing that the same be of the greatest charge and highest moment, as tending not only to the service of God, the safety of our sovereign, and discipline of our own shire, but also to the peace and profit of every singular member, yea, and to the repose, welfare, and prosperity of the universal body of the commonwealth and kingdom wherein we live. For it shall anon appear unto you, in opening the articles of your charge, that there is scarcely anything available to these so weighty and beneficial ends whereof the care is not wholly or partly recommended to you and us, either by the commission itself (in virtue whereof we sit) or by such statutes as be adjoined and do go hand in hand with it. And therefore, if we carry any regard of the service and glory of God, or be moved with desire to satisfy her Majesty in our bounden duties, or will show ourselves ready to resist such as do impeach the common good, or do retain any love of the security either of our neighbors or of ourselves, it behooveth us all and every most earnestly to employ the best powers of our minds, understandings, and wills for the execution of these most religious and salutary laws that are provided for us.

Nevertheless, forasmuch as you there and we here have not all one and the same parts and duties in this doing, since it properly belongeth to you to make inquiry and presentment, as it appertaineth to us to hear of and determine such transgressions as shall be discovered by you, wherein also you are to go before and to lay the foundation of our workmanship, I will for the present rest and rely only upon that which ought to come from you, as without the which all endeavor and whatsoever labor on our part, be it never so serious, shall prove to be merely vain and unprofitable.

It is requisite, therefore, that your inquiry be attended with a single and sharp sight, not looking through your own fingers but piercing into other men's offenses; not bleared by affection nor blinded by corruption but well cleared by the zeal of justice and wide opened for discovery of evildoers. Your presentment likewise ought to be sincere, faithful, and indifferent, without concealing any fault for favor or conceiving any for displeasure but truly either from your own knowledge or credible information of other men's oaths, wherein also you are not to be guided by that which you may fantasy to stand with good conscience but must level your whole presentment by the right line of law, according to that which you shall receive in evidence, knowing that, as thereunto you are sworn in the sight of God and men and are therefor employed in the same her Majesty's service, so must thereof make the account to God, your prince, and your country. For you may well presuppose, if you will, that you be placed for the present in the watchtower of the commonwealth and that you be, as it were, so many scouts and espies, drawn together for intelligence out of diverse and dispersed dwellings; and then, if you shall not ring the alarm nor make sign when offenders (the enemies of the commonwealth) do approach to invade, what do you less than betray your country, which you profess to defend and maintain? Or, if you will not espy these so apparent hills and huge mountains of vices that nowadays do overshadow all, are you not more than willfully and wretchedly blind and ignorant? Think it not enough, therefore, to patronize your proceedings by that usual negligence which others in your places have committed before you; neither esteem it a small thing to be put in trust and employed in the most weighty services of your native country; much less deceive yourselves in weening that all shall be well when you that carry the remedy of all in your own hands will not move so much as one finger towards it.

Oftentimes have you seen that no small number of our nobility, knighthood, gentry, and valiants of the land have not spared to expose their honors, lands, and lives to all manner of perils abroad for the only defense of us at home. And will not you afford this small time and travail, wherein is none adventure of lands or goods, and much less of limb or life, for the preservation of yourselves and your country against the secret invasion of vices, a sort of inward and domestical enemies, which do kill and slay no less perniciously than do the foreign foes? What shall it benefit us to be defended from the one if we suffer ourselves to be devoured of the other? For in vain be arms abroad if there be not order and government at home. Again, you know well with what charge, labor, and travail of purse, body, and mind, the prince, lords, and commons of the land have now lately been assembled and after long continuance in council have concluded many most necessary and wholesome laws, especially those which be ordained as well for the punishment and extirpation, if it may be, of runagate rogues and counterfeit servitors, for setting to work the able idlers at home, and for the comfortable relief of the truly poor and impotent: with all which sorts of people we have long been so extremely both charged, pestered, and despoiled that every man of us hath groaned for grief of the intolerable evil. But here again, what good have we by laws if they beget not good manners? Or what booteth it to complain of vices if correction be not applied for amendment? And now the execution of all these also is brought home to your very doors and the help put into your own hands, wherein if you shall still stand careless and secure I can say no more but that you are certainly to expect that the evil shall be wholly upon the heads of yourselves and of your own children.

For an end, therefore, since the remaining business may not afford longer time to any preface, cast within yourselves, I pray you, what it is to call God, as you have now done, to the witness of your doings; consider with what alacrity and obedience you ought to undertake her Majesty's business; bethink you how much and deeply you are indebted to the country which hath borne and bred you; and, finally, weigh the worth of your own present rest and prosperity with the change thereof and peril of the public weal which must needs ensue if your remissness be yet still given to the wicked so as they may prevail against the good and peaceable. This if you shall do, then will you not lightly run over these so great and important duties nor think it much to impart this small part of your time for the attaining of so great a good. But you will rather strive and strain yourselves to counterpoise this your business with agreeable care and diligence to the end that God may be pleased with your endeavor, her Majesty may take contentment in your travail, your diseased country may find help and cure by your hands, and your own good names and credits may be preserved both safe and unblamable, all which and whatsoever other good things I wish unto you.

Thus much generally said for preparation of your endeavors, and therefore I come now to the particular information of your minds in the articles of your charge:

ॷ

At the Quarter Sessions
At Maidstone, *17 April 1599*

It is both universally true and infallibly to be maintained that in every our advised actions of whatsoever sort the end thereof is first and foremost in the purpose and plotting, howsoever the same doth, and must of necessity, come last in the work and performance. For if in the very beginning of our enterprise we behold not the desired end and set not that up as a mark before our eyes towards which we may aim and direct the arrow of all our proceeding, we shall not only shoot far wide and lose our labor, but as each attempt will sort to one effect or other, so shall we be in danger to do harm where we intended good.

The same is therefore a most agreeable motive for us, even now in the first entry of this our no less dutiful than ordinary service: to cast the eye of our mind upon the end for which we are assembled and come together, the which no doubt is, or ought to be, for the propagation of the true religion and fear of God, for the manifestation of our own obedience to our most lawful and gracious sovereign, for the continuation of the universal good of this our nurse and native country, and for the preservation of the particular repose and tranquillity as well of our own persons and of the persons of our wives, children, familiars, and friends as of our proper goods, possessions, inheritances, and freedoms of whatsoever sort and condition against all the injuries, attempts, and acts of evil-disposed and wicked men. Than the which I know not how anything can be either more acceptable to God, more serviceable to her Majesty, more comfortable to our neighbors, more needful for the times, more available to us, or important for the matter [it]self.

The means that may lead us to effect these so great and beneficial ends be twofold: first, the laws themselves which, as they be footed upon the rock of God's truth, sided with the best reason and policy, and backed with all requisite authority and power, so do they sufficiently both enable us and warrant our proceedings upon them; then be the laborers and officers that must use and administer these laws as the most apt instruments to effect that work and end for which they are sent and put in trust, and the same be either judges or ministers, of the which first sort be you and we, for since nothing is to be done by us but according to that which shall be found by you, ye be more than half judges with us. Of the latter sort is the sheriff, the clerk of the peace, the rest of the ministers here, and so many besides as will serve the court by information against offenders.

Now for me to speak in commendation of the laws or to set forth the benefits of justice were but to gallop a field so wide and large that I might sooner run myself out of breath than half peruse and coast it. And speaking to men that can turn their faces no way but they must needs see the fruits thereof and do continually most sensibly taste and feed thereof were but to beat the air and wastefully to spend my wind. And therefore, as there is more need for us all to be admonished of the duty than to be instructed in the knowledge of this service, so mean I accordingly to address my speech, trusting that without offense of any I may put us each one in mind of that which for the furtherance of the services of this kind I take to be required of us.

I have, not without grief of mind, observed, after some long experience, that these our sessions of the peace be only formal and for fashion's sake, that our presentments also be not many and the same cold and without any zeal of justice, as being undertaken rather for private revenge than for any public good, the fault thereof resting partly in ourselves that change not the course, partly in the sheriffs that furnish not the place with more sufficient jurors, and principally in the jurors themselves that seem to put off their good consciences when they put on their clothes to come to the service. So as, if the matter were truly summed up, the total of our travail hither would appear both small and unprofitable. The remedy of all which is not only at hand but in our own very hands, so as we shall be found altogether unexcusable if we will not take and apply it.

I wish, therefore, first, that none be suffered to occupy the place of constable over an hundred but such only as can both write and read and is withal assessed to the subsidy at 6 or 8 *li.* lands, or at the double thereof in goods at the least, to the end that by the one he may be able to read and write warrants without discovery of his enjoined service to any other for their help therein, which is the breakneck of many a good business, and by the other he may be sufficient to answer for his fault, seeing that at this day nothing more than beggary emboldeneth to offense. And thus shall your great inquests be much the better peopled. Secondly, touching the particular juries of the hundreds, I take it fit that we ourselves within our special divisions do take knowledge of the most honest, discreet, and otherwise able persons, and from each part do recommend some of their names to be returned by the sheriff, lest otherwise his calendar of favorites do yet still conceal the best of that kind from us. Lastly, considering the loads of statutes that continually are increased and for execution laid upon our shoulders, I suppose it would do well that from time to time conference were had amongst us and distribution made of such of them as shall for the time be found most needful and serviceable. But as these points are not presently to be performed, so do I but only point at them, submitting the same, or the consideration of any such others, to the censure and good care of the bench here.

In the meantime, I heartily pray you now sworn of the inquests that you will forsake the trodden path of your predecessors in the place and not pattern your proceeding by the last [67] of their negligence, who, thinking it enough to have showed and ranged themselves with their fellows here, have most commonly departed leaving the service undone, whereby both offenders of all sorts have taken boldness and the country in every part and member thereof hath languished of many most grievous and almost incurable maladies. But as you have taken upon you the oath and charge, so also undertake the care and labor for the time; as you have filled the place, so also endeavor to fulfill the service; and as you have understanding and eyes, so stick not to inquire and search; and as you cannot but everywhere meet with offenses, so fail not to present the same readily that they may receive both hearing, judgment, and correction, according to their sundry degrees and qualities.

Spare not for love, dare not for hatred, stick not for fear of any to make your presentment, but simply, as out of the sight of men and yet in the sight of God, in duty to her Majesty, for love of your country, and with care of yourselves and yours, make faithful discovery of these evildoers, to the riddance of

[67] *Last:* shoemaker's last.

some of them, the amendment of others, and ease of the place where you live and dwell. So shall you both honor God, satisfy the service, recomfort us, and acquit yourselves.

W. LA.

ლ

For the Quarter Session
At Maidstone, 1 April 1600

If we would now and then for the common good and public benefit of our country bestow but some small portion of that care and cark which we daily and hourly afford to our proper business and particular profit, we should soon perceive the fruit of our endeavor, and might find that not only our part and share of the general booty would be much amended thereby but also that even that our own private gain for which we so strive with all our strength should from time to time increase and be multiplied upon us. For hereof it cometh that wickedness and contempt of good laws doth so boldly lift up the head and hopeth to prevail, to the discomfort of every member and danger of the whole body of the commonwealth, because every man almost greedily attendeth his own particular and, in manner, no man intendeth to serve the public, little weighing that his own profit is so fast conjoined with the good of other men that if he neglect theirs his own also must of necessity decay and perish therewithal.

If private men, I say, were but half so vigilant to espy out murderers and felons abroad and to draw them to public justice as they be careful to lock and bar their own doors against them, they might with less fear and peril possess their lives and enjoy their goods, yea, though they left their doors and windows unshut and wide open. Again, if public officers would vouchsafe but a little pain to see idlers set to work, to cause wanderers to be sent to their proper seats, to make unlawful gamesters to be bound from their play and disordered victualers to be presented and punished by the forfeiture of their bonds, then would not their offices be so laborious and irksome as nowadays they are become, when, seeing the burden thereof heavy by the negligence of other men, they faint before they once feel it and, despairing to discharge their whole duties, they also forslow it in each part and neglect it altogether. Finally, if jurors and inquirers would use their eyes and reveal their secret knowledges but only these four set times in the year concerning offenses that be daily and hourly committed within their own view and understanding, it were to be hoped that after a while they need not be troubled so much as twice in the year and thereby spare both the cost and travail which they now sustain.

But so is the matter nowadays handled that it fareth with the commonwealth as it falleth out with the natural body of a man, in which, whilst the hand will reach for itself only, the foot will move for itself alone, and the eye will watch but for itself and not for the rest of the members; by this unkind partiality the stomach wanteth, the sinews shrink, the blood wasteth, the vital spirits do fail, and of necessity the whole body, and therewith each of these parts themselves, do pine away and totally perish. Even so, when private men think that the care of faults public belongeth not to them, when constables are but concealers, borsholders are not busied [68] in their offices, and jurors do but juggle with their oaths, but in the meantime seducing papists, thieves, extortioners, usurers, engrossers, and the rest of that rabble have liberty to play their parts, what may we

---

[68] Much of this sentence down to this point is interlined in minute writing, much crowded, in places virtually illegible; in particular the words "care of faults public belongeth" are less than certain.

look for but contempt of laws, corruption of manners, confusion of degrees, and, finally, the conversion, or rather eversion, of this our most ancient and renowned policy?

Seeing, therefore, that the recourse of the time hath now again called and brought us together, both for the honor of God, the service of our prince, and amendment of the estate of our country by a true delivery of justice, to the encouragement of well-disposed persons and correction of such as be evil-minded, we ought each one to stir up other and so to demean ourselves in our place and function that in this our action the glory of God principally may be promoted, the princely authority of her Majesty maintained, the wholesome laws of our land rightly administered, and the good of us all both private and public spread and conserved.

And for that you that were now presently sworn must be the principal actors in this business, as upon whose hands the game chiefly resteth, I am by order and of necessity to turn myself unto you and with all hearty desire to solicit you heedily to apply your minds and endeavors to the performance of the service for which you are summoned and stand before us. Before all things, therefore, know ye that as the laws be the life of the commonwealth, so is execution the very life and soul of the laws themselves. For laws without execution are but dumb elements, books of babies,[69] rods without hands, and corselets without bodies to wear and use them. Assured we are that if laws be duly administered they be the very walls of our country and commonwealth. But what walls, though of brass itself, be not expugnable if there be not men to defend them? Understand ye also that offenses (the intestine, and therefore also the most dangerous enemies) cannot without discovery and presentment be heard and tried, without trial they may not be adjudged, and without judgment there may be no lawful execution awarded

[69] *Babies:* pictures in books, perhaps especially cupids and small figures in woodblock headpieces and tailpieces, were called "babies."

against them. And so without you, whose proper office it is to discover illdoers by way of presentment, the life of the law and consequently the very life and soul of the commonwealth itself cannot long be maintained. If you will not, then, bewray yourselves to be the murderers of your native country, the most cruel parricide that man may commit, bewray these offenders by whom it is most certainly in danger to be murdered.

Have no communion nor counsel with them that, conspiring the violation of their country laws, cannot but therewithal bring ruin and destruction to you and yours also. Imagine, therefore, I pray you, for this time that you are used as the harriers, hounds, or spaniels of the commonwealth, uncoupled and shaked off purposely to find, spring, retrieve, and unkennel all such savage beasts, noisome vermin, and ravening fowls as in their distinct natures do hurt and despoil the meek lambs, the profitable sheep, the well-occupied bees, and laboring oxen of the country. Be not closemouthed, run together, hunt not counter, quest and open boldly, follow the game and chase that you shall have on foot without change, and faint not till you have caught and killed it, which otherwise will not give over till it have killed you. Suppose yourselves, if you will, to be a politic Argus or body that hath eyes in every part and member thereof, as indeed you are a company selected for sight out of every quarter of the shire, and wink not willfully (a blindness beyond all other), but look wide and broad open, use the benefit of your sight, and no doubt but you shall soon find out and espy abundant matter wherewith both to supply the service, to busy your own conference, and to hold us at work.

For such is nowadays the bold sway of disobedience to law that it creepeth not in corners but marcheth in the open market, and is not only to be seen plainly of such as have any eyes at all but is become in manner palpable and to be felt of such as be utterly blind. Yea, such is the inundation of wickedness in this last and worst age that if speedier help and hand of justice be not applied, we are justly to fear that we shall every one be overwhelmed thereby. For albeit every man of us feeleth more or less the present evil, foreseeth further danger, feareth the end, and complaineth of the case; yet how few are there found amongst us that will use the bridle of authority which they have in their own hand and cast it upon the head of this unruly monster! Rather we are brought to this slavery that most men, both private and public, are afraid once to attempt it, the one sort for doubt of some particular mischief that thereby may befall him, the other for saving that cost and labor which the matter requireth; and so by the one and other the horse runneth away with the reins and rider, like enough to overturn both cart and carriage. God grant that this our remiss and loose dealing be not ominous and presage not the period of the English honor and translation of the kingdom. For turn over the histories both divine and profane and you shall not find that any nation hath been destroyed but that evermore iniquity hath first prevailed there and opened the way for destruction. And as we have these intestine enemies within our own bowels at home, so have we little hope of good from abroad, being bounded with old Spain and the rebellion of Ireland on the west, with the inconstancy or rather neutrality of France on the south, with the new-planted Spain in Netherland on the east, and, if you believe the old byword, with nothing but naught on the north.

Is it not, therefore, more than high time that we awake out of this sleep of security; that we send up our best prayers to God, practicing and promoting the truth of His religion; that we advance the honor of her Majesty, wishing unto her all and aye-lasting prosperity; that we constantly maintain the good laws and policy of her land, boldly putting the same in execution; that we no longer possess these places in vain nor be afraid of evildoers but that we make them afraid of us, and if by lenity we cannot win them as we would, then by severity of pains and punishment we subdue and keep them under as we ought. Especially at this and such other like-appointed times, you and others of your place must take godly courage unto you, remembering that you are not born for yourselves only but for your country also, in which you are born and bred; that you have a special credit and confidence reposed in you which you ought to answer; that you have taken a solemn oath and must receive a great charge whereof you must yield an honest accompt; and that it resteth chiefly in your power to bring medicine and amendment to all this grief and malady. So doing you shall make it to appear that you grovel not altogether for your own gain but do retain some kind affection to the common good; so shall you remove the evils that presently do annoy us and prevent the perils wherewith we are much threatened; so shall yourselves be well acquitted in this duty and others by your example shall be stirred to follow as you shall begin to lead them.

❧

For the Easter Quarter Session
At Maidstone, 1601. Not used

Of what use and importance it is in every our enterprises even at the first to set up before our eyes (as it were for a mark) the last end of our desire and action, it may easily appear to so many as understand that, howsoever the end of any business do fall out last in the execution (as doth the arrow which lighteth at the mark), yet is the same evermore the very first thing in our purpose and the chief cause and motive of our whole attempt, drift, and upshot. For if the bodily eye concur not with the hand at the first, and the fore-eye of the mind with the action

145

in such doing,[70] we may be assured not only not to hit the mark whereat we should have aimed, but (shooting awry) we shall both lose our labor and pleasure and in the end light unhappily upon somewhat that [71] we never thought for.

So necessary, then, is the foresight of the latter end that without it our whole proceeding and pains shall be either hurtful or unprofitable. Considering, therefore, that we are now brought together by order for the execution of a service no less needful for the time than profitable in use, I mean the advancement of religion in the church and suppression of many injustices in the commonwealth, let us examine the very ends thereof now at our first entry, that in all our moving and proceeding we may level by the same and make them both the guide of our journey, the butt of our desire, and the reward of our labor and painstaking.

Of these ends, then, some be more remote and farther from us and others be more near and at hand with us. The uttermost and endless end of all our actions ought to be the glory of the high God, from whom, as only author and fountain, all true both religion and justice do flow and fall unto us. The nearer end is the outward peace and profit of the church and commonwealth of our country. But the nearest and next of all is the singular good of every of ourselves, as well in our own persons as in the persons of our wives and children, our families and neighborhoods on every side and round about. For even as of necessity we are here for the time to live, converse, and have intercourse one with another, so if we shall be careful for ourselves only and careless touching others, there is little or no hope that we shall find and enjoy a civil, honest, and peaceable life with them.

[70] This clause, none too clear at best, is complicated in the manuscript by a confusion of carets; it is possible that Lambarde intended the phrase "at the first" to follow *action* rather than *hand*. The reading of *the* in "with the action" is something short of certain.

[71] Lambarde first wrote "light upon that which we . . ." and then inserted *Unhappily* and *somewhat* with carets; we assume that he intended to delete *which* when he made the other change, and we accordingly omit it.

And therefore, for the achieving to all these ends at once and with one same labor (the which, howsoever they be as far different as height, baseness, and mediocrity, yet will they readily concur in equal harmony), there is only requisite *obedience—obedience*, I say, to the religion of God, and obedience to the godly policy of our country. That inward persuasion of the mind and inclination of the heart is taught by the divines, whom God hath given us for the physicians of our souls, and is a service reserved to God Himself. But the external and professed obedience, both to religion and policy, is taught and required by the laws of men and is due (for God) to our prince and country, and is indeed the very subject and matter of this our present employment here. For as the minister of the word soundeth the inward heart, so doth the magistrate and minister of the law exact the outward sign and testimony of a well-persuaded mind. And in both these one same sincerity and singleness of obedience is required as equal and common unto them. For in religion God will have no partner of His divine glory or worship, and in policy (whereof the prince is head and viceroy, or rather vice-dieu, of God) all royal obedience is due to her Majesty alone and to such as be substituted underneath her. So as in religion it is utterly unlawful for the servants of God to erect any golden calf or other idol and to transfer unto it the honor that ought to be proper to God alone, and in policy it is not sufferable that subjects should set up any glittering calf of Rome, of Spain, of Norfolk, or of Essex [72] and to communicate thereunto that royal, obedient, and filial love which they owe to their natural prince, the mother of our country and earthly God over us.

This obedience, being planted and taking root in our hearts, will draw unto it a longing desire to see and enjoy the fruits thereof which, as they cannot be had without the execution of the laws (for none but good men be laws unto themselves), so it behooveth us as private men to practice them in our own

[72] Norfolk and Essex, leaders of rebellions against the Crown. Essex had been executed February 25, 1600/1601.

147

persons, and as ministers put them in ure upon other that be within our charge, doing the parts of good bailiffs and receivers who are not only to acknowledge the receipt that hath been committed into their hands but also to acquit themselves in an honest and true employment of the same.

Now, as the matter standeth in this case between you and us, our office it is to direct you where you shall doubt with our best advice, to hear you with all readiness when you will speak and present, to deliberate, determine, and deliver or punish according to the right of that which you shall set before us. Again, your part and duty requireth of you to inquire with your best knowledge and diligence, to utter and open that which you shall find with all indifferency and singleness, and not to conceal the faults, either of any of us sitting here or of yourselves standing there, and much less of others that be not present with us. For your oath hath none exception of persons; your duty and charge is one and the same towards all; the authority of the prince and power of the law under which you serve is general and can never be satisfied by any omission or concealment.

Consider, therefore, the malicious iniquity of this present age, which, taking the bridle in the teeth, rusheth out and runneth on to all dissolution, and therefore requireth more vigilancy in officers than any former times. Remember that you take upon you the places of men trusted with the common good, which if you shall possess in slothful and cowardly silence you shall do great and grievous wrong both to her Majesty, the law, and your native country. Cast the eye of your understanding round about you and you shall perceive that you shall neither lack matter whereupon to work, nor direction whereby to hold you in the way, nor power to prevail in this just desire, nor assistance to succor and second your endeavor, nor, finally, any other thing requisite to the effecting of this enjoined [73] service, unless you shall be found defective and wanting to yourselves, a fault

[73] *Enjoined:* the manuscript reads *enoyned.*

which, as it exceedeth all others in gravity and degree, so will it draw upon you the blemishing note of infamous persons, the displeasure of the high God, the just offense of your sovereign, the danger of the laws, and deserved detestation of your country and countrymen, whose hope shall be thus defrauded and their cause betrayed by you into the hands of evildoers that be the professed [74] enemies of the public good.

That these evils, therefore, committed by others or imminent to yourselves, may clearly be avoided or prevented, I must end as I began, desiring and entreating you to set up the end of your calling and doing as a mark before you, always retaining the same in the eye of your mind, even from your first entry through your whole labor and proceeding until the last step of your whole doing: I mean the glory of God, the general welfare of your prince, the church, and commonwealth, and the particular profit of every of yourselves and yours.

[74] *Professed:* it is possible that Lambarde intended to delete this word as he in part did, along with another (now illegible) following it.

CHARGES TO JURIES AT
SPECIAL SESSIONS AND
TO SPECIAL COMMISSIONS

Charges to Special Sessions and

Commissions

ॐ

[Speech at a Special Session of J.P.'s]
Charge for the Riot of Cutting the House
*   at Longsoleshothe*
22 March 1581 [1582], at Maidstone

Locus communis in domorum excisores [75]

The * complaint of an evil deed, good neighbors, hath moved
us to call you hither, to the intent that the rather by your good
mean and assistance we may understand the truth of it and,
understanding it, may apply such remedy as her Majesty hath
by commission and law put into our hands. I know that offenders

---

* Marginal note: *Exord.*

[75] *Locus . . . excisores:* commonplace on the cutting down of houses.
In the language of rhetoricians a commonplace is a leading case cited as
a precedent, or a case suitable for such citation. Lambarde uses the term
here presumably because the offense in question was so strange as to be,

of this kind might receive more condign punishment in some places of higher hearing, as before the lords in the Star Chamber, or before their Honors of the council board. Nevertheless, because the law chargeth us, under no small pain, to make inquisition of the fault within due time, and because also, as I think, either the doers or devisers of this act are our own countrymen and neighbors, upon whom if some moderate correction may be laid here there is hope that both they shall [be] amended and others well taught and warned thereby, it falleth out, no less for their ease in punishment than for our excuse in duty, that the matter is not carried over the pale of our own country.

The * complaint is that upon Tuesday was sevenight, being the 13 of this month, in the nighttime sundry persons to the number of twenty or twenty-four (whereof some were on horseback and some on foot) did come to a house at Longsoleshothe, lately builded by Mr. Thomas Culpeper upon his several and proper land there, wherein a poor man and his wife do inhabit, and there most furiously assailed it with axes, laboring to hew it down by cutting in sunder the corne[r] posts and principal supporters of it: which also they had brought to pass had not the building been very thick and substantially timbered. And not contented that they failed of their desire, they cast out most opprobrious speeches against the gentleman himself, threatening that if he would not within short time remove the house, that then they would soon after kindle a fire to consume it.

---

in his words, "unthought of in our laws." The following passage from Elyot's *The Governor* (1531) throws some light on this term and also on the other terms of rhetoric that he set in the margins of this charge; it comes from Bk. I, ch. xiv, where Elyot is speaking of lawyer's pleadings: "Moreover there seemeth to be in the said pleadings certain parts of an oration: that is to say for *narrations, partitions, confirmations,* and *confutations* . . . they have *declarations, bars, replications,* and *rejoinders;* only they lack pleasant form of beginning, called in Latin *exordium.* . . . Also in arguing their cases . . . they lack very little of the whole art, . . . having almost all the places whereof they shall fetch their reasons, called of orators *loci communes.*"

* Marginal note: *Narrat.*

Charges to Special Sessions

This [*] behavior of theirs, how mightily it fighteth, not only with the good positive laws of our own country, but also with the law of nations, or of mankind itself, you may easily see if you do but once cast the eye of your mind upon it. For whereas men, being reasonable creatures, have according to the law of nature always provided houses, as well to shroud them against the injury of the air as also to sever and save them from the company and hurt of beasts, these men, belike, would unhouse us and, changing nature, to become savage, and to couch and lodge with cattle in the open field. And whereas the statute laws of our realm have always taken care for the continuance and increase of dwellings, these men take in hand to overthrow dwellings, and that in this time and age wherein (considering the continual increase of people, by the sound health and constant peace of the land) it is more than necessary, and high time, to erect and multiply dwellings.

Truly, whether you will weigh and consider their fact in the nature of the deed itself, or in the manner and circumstances of the doing thereof, you shall find just cause to condemn it as very strange and barbarous. To hew down a house with axes (especially, living and Christian bodies being in it) is a thing, so far as I know, not only not read of in our histories but also unthought of in our laws, and therefore only no special punishment hath been hitherto appointed for it, because our lawmakers not hearing that it had happened before their time did not think that any should be afterward found of so beastly and savage mind as to commit it. I remember that Canute, sometimes a king of this land, doth in his laws accompt the violent breaking into a house, though it were by day, amongst those faults for which he would admit none other amends but the death of the offender. But for so many, in the night season, to assault a house standing alone and a few persons in it, with such instruments as these are, and to endeavor not so much to enter into the house as to overturn it, and that with so horrible threats and sudden and un-

[*] Marginal note: *A contrar.*

wonted fear that the poor souls within must needs be perplexed with fear of cruel death on every side, knowing that to come out of the house was to run into the mouths of these wild beasts and to tarry within was to be oppressed with the fall and ruin of it —these circumstances, I say, do so aggravate their offense that in good judgment they make it heinous and crave a law of double death, if that might be, for punishment of it. For,* if a rope be provided for him which in the daytime taketh never so little money from the person of another, though he offer no hurt to his body, then how many ropes, think you, deserve they that in the night season, with most dreadful word and act, go about to take from a man, not a little money, but his house and dwelling (a matter of inheritance), and that with the extreme hazard of the lives of sundry persons in it.

What † they meant hereby God and themselves do best know. But we may well conjecture that they sought, like giants and centaurs more than like Christian or civil men, in contempt of God and good laws, to satisfy their mischievous lusts, and that by their own wills they would have none other law remain but *legem manuum,* the law of their own busy heads and unhappy hands.

Faults ‡ proceeding of infirmity do more easily obtain pardon, and force is more tolerable where right doth go and lead it before. But these men, not pretending so much as made any color or challenge of right, have long since of mere prepensed malice conceived this monster, which also they have now at length brought forth with such sleight and cunning that they may be well thought to have been of long time taught and exercised in some school of contriving mischief. Which things § considered, as there is no man, I trust, that will think them meet to escape unpunished, so your part and duty specially at this time it is, good neighbors, with all possible endeavor to make inquisition

* Marginal note: *A Comparat.*   † Marginal note: *Ab exposition.*
‡ Marginal note: A digression conjectural.
§ Marginal note: *ab exclusione misericord.*

after them, as knowing that you shall do both rightly for them, lawfully for yourselves, and serviceably for your country, to bring their fault to light and themselves to punishment by it. For,* as there can be nothing more just than to bring the due revenge of law upon wicked and licentious persons that have against law executed their undeserved malice upon the good and honest; so also is it most lawful for you, being orderly called and charged upon oath, to find out that which they would fain hide; and right serviceable it shall be both for yourselves and all the country that by the discovery and punishment of this outrage all doors † and windows may be shut against the like malefactors, who otherwise (emboldened by impunity and this example) may unhappily enterprise some other thing that may prove not only more offensive to God and more grievous to good and quiet men but also dangerous to the blessed estate of this land and infamous for this our shire with all posterity.

I pray you, therefore, good neighbors, apply your minds with all earnest diligence and secrecy to discover the authors of this so great an evil, assuring yourselves that how much the more zealously ye shall endeavor it, so much the more evident declaration ye shall make, as well of your fear to God and obedience to your prince and country laws, as also of your charity towards your country generally that shall be holpen [and] defended, and towards the evildoers themselves particularly that may be bettered by this your care and travail.

WILLIAM LAMBARDE

[*signature in Anglo-Saxon characters*]

Day for presentment given to the jury,
until the morning of the quarter
sessions after Easter 1582.[76]

---

* Marginal note: *a iusto, a legitimo, ab utili.*

† Marginal note: *Ab eventuro.*

[76] Lambarde amended the last digit of this date so that it looks as if a 2 had been altered to 1, but 1582 must be intended, since the Easter following March 22, 1581/82 would be March 26, 1582, four days later. The quarter sessions would be about a week after that.

℃

[*Speech at Special Session*]
To the Inquirers upon the Riotous Affray at Town Malling, which happened
1 August 1592

Lest it should seem unto you, good neighbors and friends, or to any others, a vain or needless labor for us to draw this company together, and that in this busy time, for inquiry to be made of an offense committed by a few young men (who be naturally light and unadvised) and whereof neither any great harm hath already ensued nor any further memory is like to be continued, you and they both are to understand and learn that sundry grave and just reasons do not only provoke and move us but do also charge, enforce, and bind us to undertake the service. For howsoever it be not rare that young persons do suddenly fall to undiscreet words, and from thence to dangerous blows, and happily will soon be reconciled, that hindereth not but that the faults of youth should be punished, as well for their own amendment as for the forewarning of such others as they be. And albeit that much harm was not done thereby, yet is not their fault the less who did the uttermost that they might, and withal did that whereof they little knew whether the death of some of their fellow subjects would have succeeded.

Now whether they have forgotten it or no, there is little doubt but that (if it may pass unpunished) others will both remember it and take boldness to put the like in practice. But the more proper and forcible reasons that bring us hither be these: first, our duty in oath and by office for the preservation of our country's quiet, and then the penalty of 100 *li.* laid upon every of us by the law if we do not both timely and carefully interpose that authority which we have to administer. We are come, therefore, both willingly and necessarily to find out by your labor of inquiry, and to correct by lawful authority, the actors in that unlawful and riotous affray which lately happened here, both in the open street of this town and in the public assembly of the fair itself, whereof what harms might have ensued, considering the honor and power of the persons to whom these actors did appertain, the multitude of the people then presently met together, the number of weapons then near at hand, and the ready inclination of men to join with their friends, their fellows, and acquaintances, I will not stand to discourse but do leave it to your and other men's reasonable conjecture. But I must tell you that this unjust force is truly termed *atrox et publica,* fierce and public violence, as well because thereby one subject striketh another against the public law and to the infringing of the public peace of their country, which are common to them both, as also for that he useth weapon to another use than law permitteth, and (as much as in him lieth) taketh from the magistrate that sword of common justice which God hath put into his hand and abuseth it to the service of his own private sensuality, lust, and revenge.

If any man shall be disposed to take a better view of the evil that lieth under this manner of offense, let him but turn his head a little from it and cast his eyes upon the many and manifold blessings that we all do reap by the benefit of law and justice and then shall he see, as in a glass, how foul and ugly a fault this force and violence will appear. For, as one said truly, *pace sublata leges et iudicia esse non possunt:* take away peace (saith he) and you can <neither> ordain laws nor execute judgments. And no marvel, seeing that <law is> grounded upon reason, and force is the minister of furious and beastly affection, which, howsoever it may for a time put law and reason to silence, yet how unmeet a judge it is between fellow subjects in matter of question hardly is there any man either so ignorant that he knoweth not or so obstinate that he will not acknowledge. And therefore, even as next after the knowledge of God in His Christ, there is nothing in this world either more acceptable [77] to God Himself or more beneficial to men than the exercise of good and godly laws, without the which neither nation, kingdom, city, town, or family ever might or ever shall be able long to continue and endure, so this blessing (how great and excellent soever it be) can no longer be kept and enjoyed than whilst peace (which is the main cord and sinew of law) shall be preserved [78] and whilst force and violence (which is the very hatchet that cutteth that sinew in sunder) shall be kept down and repressed. For to take sweet peace out of the land were, in a word, to pull the comfortable sun out of the sky, and to bring in furious violence were to set the world on fire and to cover men with extreme horror, calamity, and confusion.

Address yourselves, therefore, good neighbors and friends, willingly to assist us in this serv<ice   > your office is diligently to inquire of this offense and faithfully to inform us <of that> which you shall find. And herein you are for many just respects to use your best care and endeavor: first, for the duty that you owe unto God, whom in your oath you have called to witness of your doing; secondly, for the service of her Majesty, by whose gracious ministry you are enabled and may be bold to punish violence; thirdly, for the hatred that you ought to bear against this sort of offense, which is the most perilous plague of the commonwealth and may reach to yourselves if you cut it not off when it toucheth others; and, lastly, for your own preservation from the pains of law, which commandeth us both to inquire of your concealment (if you commit any) and also to certify to the lords of her Majesty's Privy Council whatsoever corruption, embracery, maintenance, and sinister practice, either

[77] *Acceptable:* written above the underscored word *pleasing.*
[78] *Preserved:* written above the underscored word *maintained.*

160

in yourselves or in others towards you, that may tend to the hindrance of lawful proceeding in this business. And although you are to accompt for your service to none other but only to God and her Majesty, whose servants you be, yet, to expel those vain fears and bugs [79] which the weak mind of man fantasyeth many times to itself, I do assure unto you that, having spoken privately with both those honorable personages whose servants are said to have been the principal offenders, I found them both tenderly grieved for the chance and earnestly disposed to have the fault punished, on which part soever it should happen to be found. Now, therefore, give good ear and you shall both hear what is to be said in proof of the offense and shall also (as the matter will offer itself) have our help and advice for your better direction.

℘

[Speech at Special Session]
Charge to the Juries upon the
Dearth of Corn [80]
1586 [1587], January 29

At Frindsbury

So great and gracious hath the tender favor and loving kindness of God been towards us of this land, good neighbors and friends, during the space of almost twenty-eight years together, that He hath no less bounteously nourished our souls with the

[79] *Bugs:* bogies.
[80] This speech was probably addressed to a jury called by special commission to deal with a dearth.

161

immortal seed and food of His holy and heavenly word than plenteously cherished our bodies with store of all things requisite for the sustentation of this present life, and hath moreover so environed and fenced them both with the wall, as it were, of continual peace and tranquillity that this present age of ours hath not only far-passed all former times of most happy reckoning that have been seen or recorded here, but hath also in such wise overflown with all manner of prosperity that it hath been and is a mirror and spectacle to all nations about of the exceeding liberality and bottomless bounty of God towards such as will bear and profess the truth of His holy name.

But such and so great on the other side hath our carnal security and unthankfulness been that very few have been found amongst us that have received these blessings as given by God and not gotten by themselves, as delivered by Him for the help of others and not to be hoarded and hidden by them, or as put into their hands with the condition to come to an audit and to make an accompt for them. But each man, in manner, hath abused the hearing of the word of God to the service of his own sensuality, and those men upon whom God hath bestowed the greatest talents of worldly increase and fed them with the fat of the land, they, of all others, have by unsatiable avarice and niggishness both dishonored Him and smothered His gifts, in such wise that in that heaped measure of the greatest plenty that ever was the common sort have enjoyed no more than a wonted mediocrity and the poorer number have no less complained for want than when the doors of heaven have been fast shut and barred up against us.

These be the thanks that we unkind men have rendered; these be the praises that we have yielded; and these be the sacrifices that have been offered by us for those so many, so great, and unvaluable blessings received of Him. And therefore God (who might justly starve us body and soul, both by the famine of His word and by corporal hunger) hath in this one last year (but in a measure of great mercy) both more nearly touched us with the danger of our precious Queen,[81] more fearfully troubled us with the charge of war abroad, and more hardly pinched us with dearth and scarcity at home than He did in all that space of twenty-seven years before, mercifully minding thereby to warn us rather than to harm us, to shake the rod rather than to beat us, and to threaten and fear us rather than to destroy or kill us, if at the least by these gentle means we may be reclaimed and brought unto Him.

And that this is so, behold the undeserved goodness of God, so seasoning the present air for the next year to come that never man saw either more store of seed put into the ground or more hope and likelihood of a joyful harvest, thereby both inviting us to return unto Him by a more charitable and brotherly use of His benefits than heretofore hath been done by us, and withal letting us to see that howsoever men shall hide, cover, or shadow His benefits, yet He alone is able to feed and give the increase. In the mean season, our most gracious sovereign, the Queen's Majesty, fearing that further punishment which God may worthily inflict for our grievous ingratitude, and foreseeing the peril that may fall upon all her good subjects by the wretched fraud and fault of a few, hath thought it expedient to take the matter into her hand, and hath therefore [82] (according to that motherly care which she beareth towards all her natural people) given order that so near as may be none of her children be suffered to cry for want of bread, but that, maugre the malice of greedy and hardhearted men, these blessings of God shall be drawn out

[81] A reference to the Babington Plot, 1586, for which Mary Stuart was in prison awaiting execution.

[82] The first part of this sentence is written in the margin as a substitute for two and a half lines which read: "In this mind and to this end it hath pleased our most gracious Queen *to be our guide, and as she is the first in place, so likewise, to show herself the* foremost in example, and hath therefore . . ." The words here printed in italics are not actually deleted, but it seems certain that Lambarde meant the deleted passage to include them.

of the secret places where they be hidden and shall be brought into the open lights of the markets ready to be distributed as the necessity of each one shall require.

And because this is a work of great labor that cannot be accomplished without the help of many hands, and to the end also that her princely desire do have the better effect, she hath in great wisdom commanded that, not cornmasters, not maltsters, badgers, or covetous farmers, but yourselves that feel of the want, the honest and meaner sort of her good subjects and none other, shall be employed in this service.

Thus you see the general cause of your calling and coming hither and the matter itself that you are to take in hand, in the execution whereof you are to use both the best diligence and fidelity that you may for the better discharge of that trust and credit which her Majesty hath reposed in you—diligence, I say, in taking care, and pain for the trying out and understanding of all such points as you shall receive in charge from us, and fidelity in making unto us a true and faithful report thereof, without concealing anything for love or favor, dread or displeasure of any person. For you must know that, howsoever you may be beneficial and favorable in your own particular affairs to your friends, neighbors, or kinsmen, and howsoever also you may be afraid to deal in those things on even hand, as it were, with men that be greater or richer than yourselves, yet in these common causes and public services you may neither give away that which is not your own to bestow nor be afraid to join with God, her Majesty, and the realm against any few which whatsoever they be yet are they but dust and smoke in comparison of them.

And now, that you may yet more particularly see what is from point to point to be performed by you, I will deliver unto you by way of article the whole estate of that which is required at your hands.

1. First, therefore, you shall inquire, etc.
2. Item, etc.

3. Item, etc.

as in the paper of articles.

These be the points wherein we are to use your helpful travail and whereof we pray you to have such care and consideration as belongeth to a service that is not only well pleasing God (whose honor shall be advanced by making the best use of His gracious gifts), but also justly required by the Queen's Majesty (whose charge and care it is to see her subjects fed and nourished), and rightly beseeming your own oath and office, who may truly accompt it a credit for you to be employed in so godly and good an action.

❧

[Speech before a Special Jury]
To the Juries, upon the Renewed Orders for
Stay of the Dearth of Corn, etc.[83]
At Strood Church, 18 December 1594

Many and weighty are the careful burdens, good neighbors and friends, which rest upon the shoulders of princes and of such as sit at the helm for government in kingdoms and commonwealths. For of them it is required not only to protect their land and people against all violence of foreign invasion and to foresee that no danger do befall them from afar, but also to give order that they do at home live serviceably towards God, obediently in the laws of [84] their government, peaceably together in conversation one with another, and plenteously provided of all things that are needful for the maintenance of a good and a happy life, the contemplation of which thing alone may well

[83] On this dearth, cf. Cheyney, *op. cit.*, II, 247.

[84] Lambarde wrote "obediently towards their government," added "in the laws of" with a caret, but failed to delete *towards*.

165

move all men to acknowledge how greatly they are bounden to God that is the author of this so safe and wholesome an institution and policy, and to their princes and sovereigns whom it pleaseth God to advance for the disposing and ordering of the same.

For, seeing that we be altogether naturally given each man to make much of himself and rarely there any one is found that will take the care for others, how singular and precious a favor and benefit is it to have such an one set over us that may and doth care no less for us all and every one than we all or any of us do care for ourselves! And in this behalf, we Englishmen have, above all other nations, a great duty of thankfulness to answer, first to God and next to her gracious Majesty, seeing that by His divine favor and her gracious ministry we have not only been continually trained up in the right religion and fear of God, and so guarded from all foreign violence as from the beginning of her reign hitherto never did enemy set his foot upon the English ground, but have also been governed from time to time by a most mild and temperate administration of law and justice, and have been retained in a most constant inward peace without almost any interruption of dangerous tumult or sedition.

Neither hath her Majesty's most tender and motherly care been wanting unto us to prevent all other our wants and necessities and to provide seasonable help and relief for them. For it is yet fresh in the memories of us all that her Majesty, foreseeing about eight years ago that somewhat by the scarcity of corn but yet more by the covetous and greedy means of such as were the masters of corn a great dearth was like to ensue, she most graciously gave order for the stay thereof,[85] so as not only the markets were more plenteously served but also the poorer

[85] The Queen's orders are printed, from Lansdowne MSS 43 f. 128, in A. E. Bland, P. A. Brown, and R. H. Tawney, *English Economic History: Select Documents* (London, 1914), pp. 374–380.

sort were sufficiently fed at home for their reasonable monies.

And now again, perceiving her kingdom likely to be likewise afflicted with scarcity of corn and grain, she hath in good time commanded the citizens of London to provide great quantities thereof from beyond the seas for themselves and others, and hath also renewed the same orders whereof so much good ensued before, adding thereto some needful enlargement according to the exigency of this present time. For the more faithful execution whereof, her Majesty [86] and the Lords have taken special care in the choice of us that are put in chief trust with the service, foreseeing that none of us be cornmasters or such as for our own gain should hinder this good and charitable meaning. So have they also commanded us to use the like discretion in the naming of you, whose helps we must have both for search and inquiry in this behalf—a policy so well devised from the first to the last as none could have been either more honorable for her Majesty, more plausible to her people, more opportune and seasonable for the necessity, or more fit and full for the matter, or more orderly framed for the manner [87] of it.

Seeing, therefore, that the very drift and end of all this labor is to provide bread (not for the rich and wealthy, who have wherewith to help themselves, but for you that be of the middle sort and have not corn to sell and for the poor that have more need than you and must buy their corn as you do), seeing also that it is her Majesty's good pleasure and liking to work by your hands and endeavor this so gracious and charitable an action, it behooveth every one of you to have care of yourselves, to have commiseration of your poorer neighbors, to give reverence and accomplishment to this her Majesty's most princely commandment, boldly and cheerfully, without fear or favor, meed

[86] The word *as,* here inserted above the line in the manuscript, is doubtless the beginning of an intended addition abandoned unfinished but not deleted.

[87] *Manner:* the reading is questionable.

or malice, bestowing yourselves to search, find out, and present the verity of these special [88] articles that are both pithily and plainly devised for your charge. First, therefore, you shall . . . (as in the thirteen articles).

🍃

A Charge to the Jury Charged to Inquire of the Rogues

At the Sessions of the Peace at Maidstone, 14 June 1582, for the Delivery of the Rogues [89]

Forasmuch as it cannot but seem strange unto you, good neighbors, etc., that you should be thus extraordinarily and besides custom called together, and that in the midst of your market businesses, I think it convenient at my first entry into this matter to open unto you both the right end of your and our coming hither and the reasons that have moved the same, as knowing that the end of every affair is first in mind and purpose howsoever it fall out last in performance and effect. Our desire and meaning is under this one labor both to rid our gaol and country of a many of mighty, idle, and runagate beggars wherewith we are much pestered, and also to rid and deliver themselves from that evil mind which they carry about with them, if either this manner of proceeding may warn them or the fear of further punishment may withdraw them from it. And hereunto sundry urgent and great causes have both drawn and driven us, whereof these be some:

[88] Lambarde first wrote *suche speciall*, then deleted *suche* and wrote above *theise fow.* We may assume that *fow* was the beginning of *fowerteen*, abandoned (but not deleted) upon the realization that the number was wrong.

[89] See above, p. 25.

Charges to Special Sessions

First, we see that these idle folks do continually by heaps and flocks increase upon us, partly by the advantage of the summer part of the year, which falleth out more easy and helpful for them, partly by means of their most damnable and beastlike conversation one with another, which still bringeth us forth new fry and brood of them, partly because they fly the whip which some other places have made against them and come to us that have not hitherto taken any order for them, and partly for that many young persons, not altogether evil at the first, beholding the ease and impunity that these wanderers enjoy, do abandon those honest labors wherewith they have been acquainted (as indeed the nature of man is prone that way) and do adjoin themselves to this idle and loitering company.

Secondly, we are touched in sorrow for the horrible uncleanness and other mischiefs that they commit amongst us, and it grieveth us that these, which be all of body apt and able to labor, and whereof the most part be of foreign shires, should eat up the bread that belongeth to the poor, aged, and impotent of our own country.

Lastly, we cannot see how otherwise than by general execution of the laws in force we shall be able either to deliver our country from these evils or, suffering the same, to discharge ourselves towards God and the Queen's Majesty.

And therefore, having sundry times assembled for conference of counsel herein, we all have at the last resolved to bend ourselves with the uttermost force of law against these enemies of all religion and policy. And albeit we be of our own dispositions very unwilling to use either cutting or searing if this sore were medicable by any salve or plaster within the box of our commission, yet, being thus drawn and driven, we have determined, first of all to whip out of our country all such of them as do not belong unto us, and then to erect a house of correction for the sturdy rogues of our own shire and therewith to provide for the relief of our own poor that be impotent either by age or infirmity.

And truly, in that we come both slowly and unwillingly to the execution of the commandment of the present laws, we show ourselves right imitators of those makers of those other ancient statutes that do concern this matter who, after the proof of many means and pains devised to reduce these idle loiterers to lawful labor, were in the end constrained to forsake all other mean helps and to fly to the uttermost punishment. For in the time of King Edward the Third,* who made the first law that I find against them, it was thought that idle and able vagabonds might be restrained from begging if other men were restrained from giving them any alms or relief. But foolish piety could not hold her hands, and therefore that good meaning brought forth no good effect. Whereupon King Richard the Second † commanded that they should be kept in prison till they could find surety for their good behavior. Soon after this the prisons were <shortly> so filled and the country so charged thereby that the same King was enforced to take order that they should be no more housed in prisons but kept in the stocks abroad till they were able to find such surety.‡ And that ordinance of his continued until the reign of King Henry the Seventh, who moreover added that they should be fed in the stocks with bread and water only, by the space of six days together.§ His son, King Henry the Eighth, seeing [90] by experience that the lenity of these former laws could not abate the number of runagate and sturdy beggars, began to draw blood of them and provided whipping for their first offense and loss of one ear for the second; and yet not so prevailing against them, he afterward proceeded in degrees of greater severity, ordaining that for the first fault the

* Marginal note: 23 E.3 ca.7.   † Marginal note: [7] R.2 ca.5.
‡ Marginal note: 12 R.2 ca.7.8.
§ Marginal note: 11 H.7 ca.2 et 19 H.7 ca.12.
[90] Lambarde first wrote "seeing that the experience of these former laws. . . ." He then altered this as here printed except that he failed to delete the now superfluous first *that*. We have dropped it, as the sense requires.

gristle of the ear should be cut away, that for the second fault the whole ear should be cut off, and that the third offense should be adjudged felony.* After him King Edward the Sixth in the beginning of his reign appointed three degrees also, but he altered the manner of the punishment, making them slaves for a time, and [91] changing the cutting of the ear into a burning or branding with a letter. Howbeit afterward in the midst of his reign the Parliament was persuaded that the former sorts of severity did withhold men from putting the laws in due execution, and therefore it repealed all laws that had inflicted the pains of death and left that only remaining which gave whipping for the first offense and cutting of the ear for the second, which lenity of theirs, what success it had we have seen by our own trial, and the publishing of the statutes made in this reign of our good Queen may further inform us, which have once more thought it meet to kill and cut off these rotten members that otherwise would bring peril of infection to the whole body of the realm and commonwealth.

And howsoever these latter laws may seem hard and sharp to some, and specially to the offenders themselves that are the unmeetest judges of them, yet forasmuch as they be grounded both upon the law of God and natural reason, neither can they be justly accused of cruelty, which after all other means do at the last denounce death against such desperate offenders, nor we rightly charged with severity that come so late and unwillingly to the execution of them. It is the general law of God, laid upon all the sons of Adam, *in the sweat of thy brows shalt thou eat thy bread,* and God so detested idleness that he would not suffer Adam whilst he was in the very estate of innocency to be unoccupied but put him into the Garden to work and till it. Again, it is the will of the holy Apostle of God that he which will not labor

---

* Marginal note: 22 H.8 ca.22; 27 H.8 ca.25.

[91] The words "making them slaves for a time, and" are interlined, but without a caret to indicate the position intended for them.

shall not eat, which is as much as if he had said, let him die for it, for if food be withdrawn the body must needs perish.

And what can be more reasonable or meet than that he which will exempt himself from the common law of labor should be deprived of his meat and drink, which is the reward of labor. I confess that in respect that they be the excellent creatures of God, made of the same matter and mold that we are, and be members of the same body with us, we ought not only to cast off humanity and to rage against them but also to reckon of them as brethren and a part of our own selves. But yet, on the other side, they cannot require that we should love them any better than we do ourselves. And who is there amongst us, I pray you, which, if he have a mortified finger, toe, leg, or arm, that will not rather abide to see it cut off and cast away than to suffer his whole body to be endangered by it?

But we are not yet come so far, neither is it our purpose at this time, to take the life from any of them but only to proceed against them by whipping and boring through the ear as against rogues in the first degree; yea, rather we heartily wish and pray that it may please God to bore and pierce their hearts with His holy spirit, so that being warned by this correction they run not headlong into the second degree, which will be their destruction, but ceasing to be any longer idle drones they may become laboring bees in the hive of this commonwealth and consequently be acceptable to God, serviceable to the Queen's Majesty, and profitable to those places to which they belong.

There remaineth then no more but that you, good neighbors, that be of this jury, do make diligent inquiry and faithful report of them, not as men led aside by that foolish piety, which (as the proverb is) destroyeth both town and city and may therefore be more truly called cruelty than pity, but as men having a right eye upon the holy religion of God, the goodly law of the realm, and the bounden duty that you owe to your own country. For so shall you please God, so shall you show your obedience to her Majesty, so shall you deliver your country from many evils, and so shall you both amend these idle folks by their own punishment and warn others by their harms.

WILLIAM LAMBARDE

[signature in Anglo-Saxon characters]

ᛏ

Charge to the Jury for Rogues
[At a Special Session of the Peace at
Maidstone]
21 May 1583 [92]

If you will a while consider with me, good neighbors, how godly, profitable, and necessary this service is for the which both you and we be now assembled, I doubt not but that you will both patiently bear to be thus somewhat extraordinarily called unto it, and also cheerfully lend us your labor and assistance for the better execution of the same.

1. The very scope and end of our travail is to put in ure against idleness those laws of our realm that be grounded upon the laws of God and nature itself. It is the general law of God, laid upon Adam and all his posterity, *in the sweat of thy brows shalt thou eat thy bread.* And God is so far from giving any allowance to idleness that he would not suffer Adam, whilst he was in the very estate of innocence, to remain unoccupied, and therefore he put him into the Garden to the end that he should work and till it. Yea, it is the express will of God, uttered by the mouth of His Apostle St. Paul, *that he which will not labor shall not eat,* which is as much as if he had said, *let him die the death,* seeing that if

---

[92] See Lambarde's entry under this date in the "Ephemeris."

173

food be withdrawn, death of necessity must ensue. Or what can be, I pray you, more agreeable to nature than labor is, *whereunto* (as the holy man Job saith) *man is born, even as the bird doth naturally fly, or the spark go upward?* [93] And what is more consonant to reason than that such as will exempt themselves from the common law of labor should be deprived of their meat and drink, which is the reward of labor? Seeing, therefore, that our enterprise is grounded upon godliness and nature, let no man either lay rigor to the charge of those that made these laws of ours or accuse them of severity that shall in dutiful sort endeavor to put them in execution.

2. Now what profit may come of this our doing it is easy and at hand to see. For, first, we shall either reform these offenders, which is chiefly to be wished, or else we shall deliver our country of those evils that do accompany them, which is not to be neglected. Secondly, by taking punishment upon such as be here, we shall either withdraw or warn others that be in danger of the same contagion. Thirdly, the good and godly poor shall find the better relief when these be taken out of the way that devour the bread of charity which belongeth not unto them. Lastly, God shall be glorified and the realm served when such as be able are set to work, as bees in the hive of the commonwealth, and not suffered to loiter, as drones that devour the fruit of other folk's labor.

3. As concerning the necessity of this proceeding, you see how these idle and evil persons do continually by flocks increase upon us, partly by the advantage of the season of the year, which falleth out now more easy and helpful for them, partly by the means of their beastlike conversation which they have one with another and which daily bringeth forth new fry and brood of them, partly

[93] A marginal note here, "Set the former, latter, and in contra," seems to mean that this and the next sentence (each marked with an initial bracket) are to be transposed. Since the meaning is less than certain, we leave the sentence order as it stands.

because they fly out of other shires that have made whips to punish them and come to us that have spared to run the course of law against them, and partly for that a great sort (not altogether evil at the first), beholding the licentious ease and impunity that these wanderers enjoy, do abandon honest labors wherewith they have been acquainted and do adjoin themselves (as indeed the nature of man is prone that way) to this idle and loitering company. And, truly, as we cannot but be touched with sorrow for the horrible uncleannesses and manifold mischiefs that these wretches do commit amongst us, so can I not see how otherwise than by severe execution of the laws in force we shall be able either to deliver our country from these evils or, suffering them, to discharge ourselves of worthy blame. And therefore, even as these laws themselves (ordained against valiant beggars since the midst of the reign of King Edward the Third through the times of six or seven several princes) have made proof of many means and pains for the reducing of them to lawful labor, and were yet in the end constrained to forsake all mild and lenitive medicines and to betake themselves to whipping, searing, boring, and hanging, so we, seeing the number of such persons daily to grow upon us and having too long and in vain expected their amendment, are now at the length enforced to put in practice the laws of our own time made for the suppression of them, and have therefore both appointed this and some other extraordinary sessions for the riddance of such foreign rogues as belong not unto us and have also at the common cost erected a house of correction here for the ordering of such other of our own shire as the law doth commit unto our charge.

4. Now then, seeing that you have both the goodness of the cause to assure you, the profit to move you, and the necessity to draw and enforce you, there remaineth no more but that you, good friends, which are returned of this jury, do make diligent inquisition and faithful report of this business—not as men holden back by foolish pity, which (as the proverb is) destroyeth both

town and city and may therefore be more truly called cruelty than pity, but as men having a right and single eye upon the law of God, the statutes of the realm, and the duty that you owe unto your own country. For so shall you both please God, testify your obedience to her Majesty, and take evil from amongst us and yourselves.

ૡ

For an Inquisition Post Mortem, etc., April 1595
[Speech to Commission of Inquiry about Concealed Lands] [94]

Forasmuch, good neighbors and friends, as the common use and daily handling of any thing(though of itself never so good and important) maketh it so familiar and easy unto us as therewithal it robbeth us of all earnest cogitation and care thereof, and so by little and little bringeth upon us a remiss and negligent execution of the same; it is therefore fit for us in all our affairs of consequence and duties of charge to use a diligent preparation beforehand, and not only to bethink us of the nature and condition of the business that we are to take in hand but also to meditate upon our own duty and charge in the [95] performance and passing of it. There is no kind of service more frequent and usual than this of the inquiry of her Majesty's tenures, nor any thing at this day that I know more carelessly clouted up, as I may say, or

---

[94] The special commissions on concealed lands are listed in P.R.O. *Lists and Indexes*, XXXVII, pp. 40 ff. Six are listed for Kent, two of them for the county, dated 11 Eliz. and 23 Eliz., the rest for areas within the county. I cannot identify Lambarde's speech with any of these.

[95] A redundant *and* follows *the* in the manuscript.

more negligently slipped over, whether a man shall respect the matter or the manner of doing the same. And therefore, lest we also fall into the same fault of loose execution which unwarily stealeth upon all men, let us in a few words first consider what the thing itself is and then examine what is our own part and duty in that behalf.

The tenure of the prince, with all the incidents thereto, as rents, oaths, reliefs, wardships, primer seisin, livery, and the rest, is no new imposition but a most ancient right; no exaction by absolute authority but a settled duty by ordinary law, as well common as statute, <a not> unreasonable demand in itself but grounded upon just cause and most reasonable consideration. For the creation of tenures began with the first distribution of lands made by the prince or head of the people amongst his subjects and followers, so as the right of tenure is of equal antiquity in this land with any law that we have, not only since the Conquest but long before, even with the first government of the Germans here, from whom both we and the Norman conquerors are descended and who be the first authors of the laws *de feodis,* or of tenures, altogether unknown to the ancient Romans [96] or civil lawyers.

Again, there is no duty or right answerable to the prince from us that is more free from irregular and absolute power than this of the tenure of our lands, which not only hath her foundation from the common law and perpetual usage of the realm, but also hath her confirmation from the law of the Great Charter and many other statutes made by the common consent of the realm and kingdom. Lastly, what can be more reasonable than gifts upon condition, since they are the very contract and agreement both of the giver and taker? Now, that the tenure is a condition of service, annexed by the first giver of the land and accepted by the first taker for himself and all such as shall succeed him, it

[96] *Romans:* the final letter is obscure; the word ought perhaps to be read *Roman.*

is manifest to all men that know what a tenure is. And if that be an allowed duty to every subject that is a lord of land over his fellow subject or his better that is a tenant unto it, how much more ought we to allow it for good and reasonable to the prince, who is not only the head of all his subjects but also supreme lord of all the lands within his rule and dominion? Shall one subject have over another the duty of fidelity, rent, heriot, relief, and wardship, and shall we think it hard or strange that the prince of the people, the head of the politic body, the father of the country, and vicar of God himself shall enjoy the like?

The matter and business itself, therefore, thus shortly showed to be not only right ancient but also most lawful and reasonable, let us take a like short view of our own duty in the execution of the same. This shall we best do if we lift up our eyes and behold the person for whom we do it, that is her most gracious Majesty, our natural prince and loving sovereign. For to inquire of tenures by writ or commission is peculiar to the prince and not communicable to any subject. The subject may find his tenure by his own tenants, but the writ out of the Chancery to the escheator and the commission out of the Wards to the persons authorized therein have the words, *qui de nobis tenuit in capite, ut accepimus*, so as it is proper to the prince alone. And therefore, as on the one side it is an abuse to the subject to press him with that [97] writ or commission for inquiry where the tenure is neither plain nor probable for the Queen, so is it on the other side a great infidelity [98] towards the service of the Queen herself to make such inquiry of set purpose to find a tenure against her. Now, with what diligence we ought to handle the affairs of her Majesty, not only for conscience sake to whom we owe all our obedience in God, but also for testification of our thankfulness for

[97] The word *to* follows here, evidently through Lambarde's failure to delete it along with other words.

[98] The words *is it* follow here, evidently through Lambarde's failure to delete them along with other words.

the great benefits that we reap by her government, as freedom of conscience, security of goods and possessions, administration of indifferent law and justice, inward peace at home, and defense against all hostility, invasion, and enmity abroad, I leave to each man's conscience and consideration, not doubting but that all and every man of us will acknowledge that we do not only stand bounden to serve her in these and the like common services with all fidelity, cheerfulness, and good endeavor, but also that we owe unto her both our hearty prayers unto God for her and the ready service of our goods, lands, limbs, and lives wheresoever she shall please to call upon us.

Thus much for preparation in general. Now for the present and particular I know not how either to win time better or to instruct you [99] sooner than by rendering the commission itself.

୧

Charge at the Commission for Almshouses, etc. Uttered at Maidstone, 17 January 1593 [1594]

You gentlemen and the rest that be sworn: I doubt not but that you have well observed that her Majesty's commission, which was even now read over unto you, standeth upon these four principles following: first, the information that her Majesty hath received that many, as well of the ancient as late provisions, charitably made for relief of the poor, are [100] nowadays most unconscionably converted to the private purses of some such as have the administration and handling of them; secondly, her Highness' most princely and Christian care to have that abuse to be speedily and severely corrected; thirdly, the special trust that

[99] *You:* the manuscript reads *your.*

[100] *Are:* the word in the manuscript is *as,* an error doubtless due to contamination from the earlier part of the sentence.

179

her Majesty reposeth in us her commissioners for the effecting of the same her royal pleasure and most godly desire; and lastly, some means and direction by way of articles for the better conveying of our labors throughout the whole service. Now, forasmuch as amongst those means we have resolved to begin with inquisition, wherein we are to use the aid and ministry of you (purposely therefor called hither and sworn), I hold it fit, as well for the preparation of your willingness of mind as for the better furnishing of your knowledges, first, to let you know that this service (wherein you are presently to be employed) is no less pleasing to God than profitable to your country, then, to let you see that there was never more need than now to have the same put in ure and execution, and, lastly, to leave with you some helps for your more easy and safe proceeding therein.

If I should labor to prove unto you that, both by natural reason, by all ancient policy, and by the present examples of other countries, we ought to relieve and keep at home our poor people, without suffering them to wander hither and thither to seek their living, I should enter into a large field, where I might find matter enough to misspend the time, to tire myself, and weary the company. But, forasmuch as the only law and word of God (which is the right rule of all our actions) ought to content us that be Christians and to be unto us instead of whatsoever reason, example, or authority, I will only draw a word or twain from thence to serve us for the present. In one same chapter of the book of the repetition of the law, you may read first this: *Omnino mendicus inter vos non esto*,[101] let there be no beggar at all <among>st you; and after that: *non deerunt pauperes, in terra habitationis tuae, ac propterea tibi praecipio ut aperias manum tuam pauperi et egeno fratri tuo*,[102] there shall want no poor in the land of thy dwelling, and therefore I command thee to open thine hand to thy poor brother, in which words there is a show

---

[101] Deut. 14:4, with deviations from the Vulgate.
[102] *Ibid.*, 15:11, with deviations from the Vulgate.

of contradiction, the one prohibiting beggars and the other prophesying that there shall be poor. But as the word of God is all truth, and the same most constant an[d] agreeable with itself, so can it admit no contradiction. And therefore, if you will understand by the word *beggar* him that goeth from door to door begging his bread, and by the word *poor* him that howsoever he needeth is ashamed to beg, these two sentences will agree in good harmony, both commanding us to open our hands for relief of the poor at home, without suffering them to gad abroad for their living, the which, as it increaseth many evils amongst them, so doth it convince us of great want of charity, pity, and compassion. Now therefore, if you be desirous to please God, how can you do it better than by obedience to His law, which Himself accompteth better than sacrifice? Again, if you seek the profit of your country you shall find it a singular profit to restrain and keep at home these swarms of vagrant and flying beggars, who do not only thereby lose that time which for the profit of their country ought to be bestowed in such labor as the abilities of their bodies will bear but do moreover infect and stain the earth with pilfery, drunkenness, whoredom, bastardy, murder, and infinite other like mischiefs.

Furthermore, if we be commanded to relieve and succor the poor, are we not also thereby enjoined to punish, by the best means that we lawfully may, all such as do rob and spoil them? *Panis egeni, vita est pauperum, et qui eum subducit homicida est:* [103] the bread of the needy (saith the son of Syrach) is the life of the poor, and he that taketh it from them is a very murderer. The rich glutton was thrown into hell for not affording from his own table somewhat to poor Lazarus. What hell then can be enough to torment them that do not only not give of their own to Lazarus, but do take from him that which is his own and proper? By which manner of wicked ravin it must needs ensue that either the poor shall starve for want or else we, you, and the

[103] Eccles. 15:25, with deviations from the Vulgate.

commonwealth must supply at our own charge that which these men have so wretchedly embezzled and taken from them, both which are great inconveniences and not tolerable in any well-governed, and much less in a Christian, country and commonwealth. Thus then you may be assured that you have in hand the service of God and the profit of your country.

Now, that there is more necessity of this help at this day than the former ages have felt there are two special reasons that will make it plain for me: the one, because the number of the poor is greater now than beforetime it hath been; the other, because there is also a new sort of poor arisen amongst us of late which in old time was not known to our forefathers. Many things there are to enforce that the number of the poor is increased, but I will note only three which I take to be above the rest: first, the increase of all sorts of people generally amongst us; then, the dearth and high prices of all things needful for life; and lastly, the dissolute education of the brood and children of the poor. That the number of our people is multiplied, it is both demonstrable to the eye and evident in reason, considering on the one side that nowadays not only young folks of all sorts but churchmen also of each degree do marry and multiply at liberty, which was not wont to be, and on the other side that we have not, God be thanked, been touched with any extreme mortality, either by sword or sickness, that might abate the overgrown number of us. And if all, then each sort, and in them the poorer sort also, must needs be augmented.

The dearth of all things maketh likewise many poor, and that cometh either by the excessive enhancement of the rents of land, which hath now invaded the lands both of the church and Crown itself, or by that foul and cancerous sore of daily usury, which is already run and spread over all the body of the commonwealth, or by our immoderate use, or rather abuse, of foreign commodities, the which we (breaking all symmetry and good proportion) do make as vile and common unto us as our own domestical.

But whether these only, or chiefly, or they with some other be the true causes of dearth, that is a disputation for another time, place, and assembly. These I note that every man may have a conscience in them, lest through his fault dearth grow and consequently the number of the poor be increased by it.

Lastly, the poor are exceedingly much multiplied because for the most part all the whole children and brood of the poor be poor also, seeing that they are not taken from their wandering parents and brought up to honest labor for their living but, following their idle steps, be *ma<la a>vi, malum ovum*,[104] and are neither good eggs nor birds, but as they be born and brought up so do they live and die, most shameless and shameful rogues and beggars.

And to the increase of these evils, we have, as I said, a sort of poor lately crept in amongst us and not before known to our elders: I mean poor soldiers, of whom this commission specially speaketh. There were always poor leprous, poor lazarous, aged poor, sick poor, poor widows, poor orphans, and suchlike, but poor soldiers were either rarely or never heard of till now of late. And this is the reason: not only in old time but also within the reach of our own memories, at the journeys to Boulogne, Musselburgh, St. Quintins, New Haven, and Leith, the nobility, knighthood, and gentry of the realm carried to the wars with them their <fr>eehold or copyhold tenants, their able and wealthy neighbors, and their own menia<l> and household servants, of the which three sorts, two were able at their return to live of their own, and the third was never forsaken of their lords and masters under whom they had adventured. But now, when not only our gaols are scoured and our highways swept but also the cannels [105] of our streets be raked for soldiers, what marvel

---

[104] Loss due to decay is of approximately the right extent to suggest the restoration here put forward, a variant of a recorded proverb, *mala gallina, malum ovum.*

[105] *Cannels:* a word closely related to *channel* and *canal.*

is it if after their return from the wars they do either lead their lives in begging or end them by hanging. Nevertheless we are by many duties most bounden to help and relieve them, considering that they fight for the truth of God and defense of their country; yea, they fight our own war and do serve in our places, enduring cold and hunger when we live at ease and fare well, lying in the open field when we are lodged in our beds of down, and meeting with broken heads and limbs when we find it good and safe sleeping in a whole skin.

Now therefore, seeing the honesty, utility, and necessity of this present service of God, her Majesty, and your country, it importeth you to enter into it with all readiness and endeavor, following her Highness, your most princely captain and guide, who, being a queen of great majesty, showeth herself a true shepherd of her people, sticketh not to descend from her throne as it were to take this great care even for these the basest and most miserable of all her subjects; and knowing that, as they be not only men as we are but our own countrymen and brethren also in Christ with us, we ought in all humility, love, and charity both to pity their wants and to provide for their necessities. This if you will do, you shall not only please God (who will take it done to Himself whatsoever you shall do for His poor servants) and satisfy her Majesty's most godly desire (whose care you may see by her own words in this commission) but also unmask these robbers and monsters that they may be brought to punishment, and provoke the poor themselves, in whose behalf you shall travail, to pray unto God for you and us all.

It now remaineth that I leave with you some helps that are provided for your furtherance in this proceeding: first, therefore, you shall hear and then have these articles following. . . .

ॐ

For a Commission Post Mortem
November 1596

Many charges and services there be, good friends, which upon a sudden view may seem hard and heavy unto us, not so much because they be such in themselves as for that we which do undergo them do not steadfastly look into those true reasons which both at the first moved and yet do continue and maintain them. And amongst others the tenure of her Majesty's prerogative, about the which we are now purposely assembled, hath the show of a great and grievous exaction, as the which not only stayeth our hands that we cannot do with our own as we would whilst we live, but also enthralleth the persons and possessions of our children and restraineth the liberty in marriage of our wives when we be dead. Howbeit, if we would advisedly consider first to whom, then from whom, and lastly for what cause this is due and demandable, then would the burden seem not only more tolerable but also convenient, just, and necessary to be performed and borne by us. A word or two, therefore, of each of these three, that the rather thereby we may be allured to serve as we ought, that is to say, cheerfully and with all faithful diligence and endeavor.

This service, therefore, is due to the prince of the land, the vicar of God, the head of the public body, the shepherd of the people, the father of the country, and protector of so many as live under the wing of his law and obedience, by the favor of which <his> office the subject is trained in due religion, governed in upright justice, furthere<d in wea>lth, defended in all his possession, cared for when he is secure, and watched for when he is asleep, so as by the benefit of this earthly and mortal god (set over the people by the only true God that is both heavenly and eternal) they be neither disturbed in peace nor destroyed by war but do grow up, flourish, and prosper in all manner of joyful and happy success. And now, even as all these good parts are procured by a good prince, so hath the [106] most gracious majesty of our sovereign many years together most motherly provided every of the same for us, as all the world abroad doth know and we at home most sensibly do feel and enjoy. And therefore, seeing that whatsoever we have, we have it by her good means and ministry, we are taught not to think much of any duty that we yield, being generally debtors unto her not only of our goods and fortunes but also of the very bodies that we bear and of the lives that we do breathe.

But besides this general duty, which tieth us in and for all, we do owe in this particular point of our present business a more special debt even by our own contract, oath, and agreement. For, considering that in the beginning all the possessions of the realm were by the mere gift of the prince distributed amongst the subjects of the land, to be holden by sundry services, either of peace or war, and to render diverse beneficial duties therefor, not only they which first took them but we also that now derive our interests under their agreement are bounden so to hold and continue the same. And for the more assurance hereof, in all sorts of temporal tenures, we give our corporal oath, either of fealty alone or of homage and fealty together. And truly, howsoever the present possession, fruit, and profit of those land<s> be permitted unto us, yet the very dominion and right propriety thereof resteth still in the prince, which appeareth most evidently by this: that the lands of any subject in the realm shall escheat to the prince for his infidelity or treason, and so shall return to the head from whence it was at the first derived.

[106] *The:* amendment has obscured this word so that the reading is not certain.

Neither ought these things to seem strange to us nor once [107] be thought to be hardly exacted by the sovereign of all, when every inferior subject, being lord but of a small manor, reapeth some petty royalties of such his fellow subject[s] as do hold any their lands of him.

Nevertheless, as the prince is head and chief of the rest, so this tenure of her hath some preëminences above the tenures of common persons, and namely this, for one, about the which we are now employed by this present commission: I mean, to inquire by writ, or by commission in the nature of a writ, after the death of her supposed tenant, a thing not communicable to any subject how great or mighty soever he be. For albeit that inferior lords of lands may by the oaths of their own tenants inquire of such as die in their homage, yet no writ post mortem after the death of any sort is grantable but in the case of the prince alone, insomuch as it is both a great indignity to the Queen, an abuse of the office, and a wrong to the subject to procure any of these writs or commissions but only where there is some matter of record, either plain or probable, to make a tenure in chief for her.

Thus shortly you have seen both to whom we are to answer this duty, by whom it is to be yielded, <and for> what cause it is originally due and payable. It remaineth now, th<at, accord>-ing to the oath which you have taken and according to that duty which for so good reason you do owe, you address your minds to this service with all readiness and prepared good will, considering that as her Majesty is pleased to make you judges in this case between herself and her supposed tenant, so it behooveth you to apparel yourselves with that loyalty and uprightness which belongeth to judges, so as by your travails neither her Majesty do receive loss or wrong nor her subject be charged but only

[107] *Once:* the reading in the manuscript appears to be *oncy.* The whole passage is made difficult by Lambarde's carelessness in deletion and the placing of carets.

according to right and the law of the country whereof he is partner and co-heir with you.

༜

At an Office Post Mortem
May 1600

As the policy and government of this kingdom wherein we live
is a most wisely compounded temperature of the three estates
thereof: the prince, the lords, and ourselves that be the commons,
wherein each part is so rightly tuned that they do nevertheless
all join together without confusion or jar in a most sweet and
melodious harmony; so in that part which belongeth to us the
commons there is no one thing that more clearly soundeth out
our great favor and freedom than this power that we ordinarily
have in the trying and deciding of rights in suit and controversy
which the common law of our country putteth into our hands,
and wherein we have not only a certain preferment (if I may
so term it) above the nobility but also a mark of rare favor from
the very prince and sovereign. For, whereas the lords are neither
judges over us, nor (but in case of life only) do judge amongst
themselves, and the prince of the land will not be judge where
he is interested as a party, we the commons do not only try and
judge the controversies that arise amongst our own peers and
equals but also those that happen either between the nobility
themselves or between the sovereign and whatsoever subject. In
all which I may boldly say that we be the judges, because who-
soever pronounceth the judgment it is bound and must be suitable to the verdict or presentment of us that be the jurors—a
prerogative peculiar to the English nation and not permitted to
the commons of any foreign kingdom.

These things will bear discourse, and peradventure you expect

188

it, but I only propound them shortly to put us in mind, first, that in these and the like businesses you by inquiry and verdict and we by direction and advice do sustain the persons of very judges, and, next, that after a special manner we are put in trust by the law with the right that is in controversy between our sovereign head and our fellow subject, the one of which respects ought to move our indifferency and the other to draw our dutiful attendance. And therefore, seeing that we are now come together for this service of her Majesty's tenure by the prerogative, it importeth us so to demean ourselves herein as that the truth and right may appear, without either detracting from her Majesty's due or grieving the subject against her law and liking. We must, I say, neither reckon that well gotten to the subject which is wrongfully withdrawn from the prince nor gained to the Crown which is won by injustice upon the subject. But setting apart all wrong and wrenching, we must go on with even pace, equal ears, indifferent minds, and sincere consciences. For in so doing we shall not only satisfy the service and acquit ourselves of all blame, but we shall be also found worthy to use and enjoy this great freedom of our country law in virtue whereof we are now employed.[108]

[108] The manuscript has no terminal punctuation. This may be an incomplete draft.